SHADOWS ON THE CANYON WALL

VOLUME 1

MARY VISKER

Gotham Books
30 N Gould St.
Ste. 20820, Sheridan, WY 82801
https://gothambooksinc.com/

Phone: 1 (307) 464-7800

© 2023 Mary Visker. All rights reserved.

No part of this book may be reproduced, stored in a retrieval system, or transmitted by any means without the written permission of the author.

Published by Gotham Books (February 1, 2023)

ISBN: 979-8-88775-205-1 (sc)
ISBN: 979-8-88775-206-8 (e)

Because of the dynamic nature of the Internet, any web addresses or links contained in this book may have changed since publication and may no longer be valid.

The views expressed in this work are solely those of the author and do not necessarily reflect the views of the publisher, and the publisher hereby disclaims any responsibility for them.

TABLE OF CONTENTS

SHADOWS ON THE CANYON WALL VOL. 1 1

    CHAPTER 1 9
    CHAPTER 2 15
    CHAPTER 3 27
    CHAPTER 4 41
    CHAPTER 5 55
    CHAPTER 6 79
    CHAPTER 7 111
    CHAPTER 8 125
    CHAPTER 9 141
    CHAPTER 10 159
    CHAPTER 11 177
    CHAPTER 12 199
    CHAPTER 13 219
    CHAPTER 14 235

SHADOWS IN THE CAMPUS HALLS VOL. 2 249

    CHAPTER 1 251

Dedicated to the memory of my dad who

Gifted me his love of adventure and the out-of-doors.

And to my mom who taught me the wonderful

Solace of sincere prayer.

CHAPTER 1

Determination is pouring out of every cell of my body as I talk to myself. I've got to beat her! I've made it to a tied score of duce third set with "Miss Country Club". Now, just two more points and the poor little rich girl will lose her state tennis championship title.

Winning this match means more than any other I have ever played in my life. I must beat Pam! Taking a deep breath, I crouch into my receiving position about two feet behind the service line crowding the forehand side.

Pam toes the service line, looks at me, and calls out the score, "Duce".

I watch her bounce the ball her habitual two times on the ground, then pause. Her arm reaches high to put the ball up for the serve, a little higher toss than usual, followed by the swing. The ball comes bulleting over the net, but my instinct tells me to let it go. I smile when I hear the line judge call, "Fault".

I crowd the service line now and concentrate all my thoughts on the next serve. I almost think out loud. This one's mine. Her second serve will be soft, and I'll be able to put it anywhere I want. I'll kill it.

The soft serve comes as I'd calculated, and I am on top of it instantly. I send it slicing down the line to Pam's backhand and at the same time rush the net. It's almost a put-a-way, but Pam manages to get her racket on it and sends it up in a shallow lob straight to the net. I smile from ear to ear as I wait for the ball. Pam makes no effort for a save as I send it smashing on an impossible angle out the side of the court.

The school coach said it didn't matter who won this match. Either way, we bring the same points to our total team score. To me, it makes all the difference in the world. This win would be the culmination of years of hard work, and I'll feel a step closer to being somebody. If a kid who couldn't afford any lessons but just learned to play from the city recreation league can beat someone who belongs to the country club, has private lessons every day, and holds the state singles title, then this kid must be somebody. I rehearse this constant dream again as I walk, with a determination boiling inside, back to receive the last serve.

As Pam is about to begin her traditional windup, a voice from the first row of spectators right next to me splits my concentration. "Come on Pam! Get your act together! You can't let someone like her beat you! Send her back to the slums where she belongs!" Pam's dad is yelling at me five feet from where I'm standing.

Because all is settled for the serve, there is no noise to dull his message, and I can hear every syllable. Pam turns her head away from me and her parents. She takes a step away from the serving line catching a quick breath. Instant anger begins to swell in me as the words thunder over again in my mind. With anger boiling to the breaking point, I take my stance to receive. The serve comes but my swing is just a hair late, and the return goes wide. The score is back to duce.

My mind is frantic with a self-conversation. What have you done to yourself? You let them break your concentration, and then you let yourself get angry--the only thing that could beat you. You let Pam's arrogant father inside your head. Put your mind back on the ball and get it over the net.

I try hard to force the concentration for the next serve, but as luck would have it, Pam tries one of her bullets. This time it goes in. A roar goes up from the crowd as I am aced. I go back to my mental conversation, Okay. It's not over yet. Your anger is under control. Now put all your thoughts into getting the ball over the net. Keep your eye on the ball and get your weight forward. Be ready! Be ready!

As the serve comes, this time I am ready and put it back into play. The return is soft and not placed with a winner's determination. Pam sends the ball back easily. An endurance point seems to be underway as I put the ball over the net, hoping Pam will make a mistake. Without the put-away shot, I find Pam to be a solid wall who returns everything. I just can't pull the aggressiveness back; I am too afraid I'll make the final mistake. The fear almost paralyzes me. After ten or eleven returns, back and forth, my concentration thins. My thoughts move back to the comments, "You can't let someone like that beat you!" On the next return, I hit the ball into the net, and Pam wins the match.

The roar of victory goes up from the crowd. Friends, teammates, and unknown bystanders rush onto the court to congratulate Pam. I think winners always have an instant popularity boom no matter how close the competition is. I watch Pam as she accepts the hugs of congratulations for a few moments. I know I should turn toward the net for the ritual winner-loser handshake.

I am still standing in the spot where I hit the last ball, trying to control the tears and the anger bringing the tears. My brother, Tom, is now standing beside me with his arm around my shoulder, and my recreation coach has just entered the court on his way to me. I deliberate on which direction I should go. With all my heart, I want to run as fast and as far away as possible. Then with no words, I turn with fast determined steps to the net. They might have cheated me out of the match, but they are not going to chase me off the court. I reach the net before Pam and stiffly extend my hand. She gets there, takes my hand, smiles, and waits for the congratulations. Instead, we both hear the voice of Pam's dad, "Terry! You played an awesome match."

I glare at Pam, then at her father, turn, and walk away. I move quickly, a half run - half walk to my things on the sideline bench. Gathering them into an awkward pile in my arms, I head for the car. I'm almost out of the fence into the parking lot when my brother catches up with me. "Terry, that's the best tennis I have ever seen you play. You almost had her. If you hadn't choked a little right there at the end, the match would have been yours."

I want to yell or scream or something. But all I can do is let the tears run down my face, swallow hard on the lump in my throat, and walk faster. Tom is still right beside me, "Terry, what are you running away from? You played a super match. You can be proud of the whole thing. Aren't you going to stay and get your trophy?"

I still say nothing. I'm not going to stay here and take second place when Pam doesn't even think I am worth playing. Determination begins to swell out of my anger. I will never take second place to Pam again.

Still trying to keep up with me and talk at the same time, Tom tries again. "Pam is the best player I've seen for a long time. She beats anything you practice against down at the park, including the boys. You two should be practicing together; you'd both be much better players if you would. Your school coach was telling me about the National Armature Championships next fall. He said if you two would team up and play doubles, you would stand a chance of placing."

Tom's words finally get through to me. I stop dead still, turn, stare at him, and say with slow, angry, determination, "I will beat her if it's the last thing I do, and I will N-E-V-E-R, never help her win anything. Do you understand? Nothing!" Without another word, I walk even faster to the car.

CHAPTER 2

"Terry, are you up yet? I let you pretend to be sick Friday after the match, but you're going to school today."

I almost knock Tom over as I bolt out of my bedroom door with both arms full of schoolbooks and posters. "See, I'm ready, and I'm out the door. What are you waiting for?"

I can feel my dark-haired, six-foot-two brother following me down the hall and through the kitchen trying to catch my arm. I'm balancing books and opening the door when he finally catches hold of me.

"Not so fast. You still have half an hour. You haven't had breakfast, and we haven't had family prayer yet. What's the big rush? You never go this early."

I explain as I pull Tom out the door, "Some things are more important than food. I've got to be ready for American Problems, and I still have information to pick up from the health teacher." I stack my pile in the back seat and open the passenger door to the front seat. I hesitate, then run for the house calling back over my shoulder, "Get the car warmed up, I forgot my note cards."

When I return, Tom has the car started and is shaking his head. "Terry, sometimes I don't understand you. Friday I couldn't get you out of the house. Today I can't hold onto you long enough to feed you. I know you're a straight "A" student, but I've never seen you prepare like this for any class. What's going on?"

I'm way too casual in my answer, "Oh, it's nothing much. My study group in American Problems presents its report to the class today."

"You've got enough stuff there for ten people. Did anyone else in your group prepare anything?"

"They've done a lot of work, but I just want to make sure we're prepared to the max. You know, better safe than sorry."

Tom still doesn't seem satisfied. "You're not telling all. There's more to it than just a report."

"Okay, so it's a little debate. There are two study groups, and each takes one side of an issue," I explain.

A little light is dawning in Tom's eyes, "Terry, who's on the other team?"

The car is in front of the west doors of the school, and I delay my answer until I have my arms stacked high again. I turn toward the school then back to a waiting Tom, "The teacher says they're study groups and not teams. Because this is a friendly competition, it's for the education process only... Pam is on the other team." With that, I slam the door with my foot and juggle my load into the school.

Rushing down the hall with my arms full, I'm amazed a school can be so empty and lonely at 7:30 a.m. and so crowded and noisy at 7:55 a.m. A quick trip to the health room gives me the last poster I need. The next fifteen minutes are spent in my classroom hanging the charts and pictures for this "friendly debate." Having completed every preparation I can think of, I slip into my desk to collect my thoughts and wait.

I'm ready—I know I am ready. I feel a little agitation about having spent so much extra time on this project, but after the tennis match last week it will be worth it. I think about Pam and how the competition between us has always been there. Lately, it seems to be more intense, and Pam is there every time I do anything. I wonder a little why it is becoming so important for me to be the *winner* in our unending confrontations.

My thoughts shift to visualize how Pam will look as she walks into the classroom with her aura of confidence. Wearing one of her latest fashion outfits, she will be so completely coordinated there will be some accessary in her long blond hair matching her clothes. From hair and make-up to shoes, every detail will be perfect.

I smile as a ridiculous thought crosses my mind. If Pam and I were to trade clothes, they would probably fit exactly. I almost laugh out loud as I try to picture Pam in the T-shirt and jeans I have on today.

The opening door brings me back to reality. A group of about ten kids push through the limited access and fan out to their seats. Pam is in the group. I watch her take in the room preparations and allow myself one last thought. You look just like I thought you would, but just wait until this hour is through. You won't look or feel number one. As the bell rings at 8:00 AM, I feel a surge of confidence. This time Pam will walk away in second place.

"As soon as we suffer through morning announcements, we'll get our discussion started. The study groups presenting material this morning are the ones working on controlling drinking and driving." Mr. Richards is trying to start class when he is cut short by the unseen voices invading the classroom from the little mesh screen high on the wall for morning announcements.

Some mornings I wish the broadcast would take the entire period, but this morning it seems as though it will never end. They invite everyone to the schools-out dance on Friday night. Unending and unclear instructions are given to the seniors about graduation exercises. Every team which played last week is congratulated, and then the usual list of students who are to report to the principal's office for one reason or another is announced.

Finally, the blaring speaker falls silent, and Mr. Richards moves from his chair to sit on his desk. He gives instructions while motioning with his hands. "You people sitting in the front row of desks find an empty seat somewhere. Pam, you take three of these front desks, turn them around, and put your group in front over there. Terry, you take the other three desks and put your group on this side."

After a few seconds of maneuvering, the battlefield is laid out. There are two groups of desks in the front of the classroom. They are both lined up at an angle, so they are half facing each other and half facing the class.

With the teams in place, Mr. Richards lays the ground rules. "Remember, this is not a formal debate. It's just another way to help you study. Take a few minutes and make sure each person on your team knows what they're covering. When you're ready, each side will take a turn presenting its material. If we have time, we'll let the class ask questions at the end. Pam, your side starts first."

Sandy and Mark huddle around my desk making sure their cards are in order, and I give them some additional facts I gathered over the weekend. We also decide Sandy will be first, Mark, second, and I'm third. I make sure my closing statement will be last. If Pam's group is to begin, it means I will be the concluding speaker for both groups. I smile as I think to myself, this is working out better than I hoped.

Pam's group takes a little longer organization time. When they are ready, Pam stands by her desk and begins for her group. "No one wants a drunk driver on the road. We have laws now to guard against the drinking driver. The law itself doesn't seem to be keeping the drinker from behind the wheel. That would lead us to understand something different than stiffer laws are needed. The medical profession recognizes problem drinking as a medical problem and alcoholism as a disease. You don't take a person with epilepsy and put him in jail if he has a seizure while driving.

You care about the whole person and treat the disease so the person can function as normally as possible. Jail terms and fines do not promote healing. What the drunk drivers need are education, treatment, and rehabilitation."

The whole class buzzes when Pam finishes. Sandy reflects their feelings as she leans over and whispered to me, "That's a tough act to follow. What should I do?"

I smile to myself as I think, Pam, you've done your homework. That's okay so have we. With reassuring confidence dancing in my brown eyes, I whisper back to Sandy, "Don't worry. Give the information just like you have it. She's good, but we're in good shape too. Just be confident!"

Sandy stands tall, looks the other team straight in the eye, and begins her delivery. "I think we need to look at cold facts for a moment. One-third of all highway deaths involve alcohol. Let me make this point a little plainer. During the ten years from 2006 to 2016, ten thousand people were killed every year in drunk-driving crashes. Every year since then the numbers have increased, but the percentage says the same. About one-third of all highway deaths are alcohol-related. If there were stiffer laws and penalties, people would think twice before they drink and drive."

Eric from Pam's team is on his feet fast. "You're right about the use of alcohol and related deaths. Over thirty percent of highway deaths do involve alcohol. But you should also be aware that 34% of those are caused by problem drinkers or alcoholics. If alcoholics were forced into treatment, they would be helped, and the drunk driving problem would be helped too."

From that point, the debate moves on with a fury. Each person is on his or her feet with new information almost before the other team is finished. It is almost becoming a game to see who will run out of facts first.

Then about five minutes before the class period is to end, my turn comes around again. This time I do not stand up but speak slowly and deliberately from my desk. "Six years ago this spring, both my mom and dad were in our family car coming home from a faculty party up at the university. They stopped for a red light on Transom Street and started through when it turned green. They were right in the middle of the intersection when a car going, the police estimate, 90 miles per hour went through the red light. My mom and dad both died within hours. The guy driving was dead drunk but not dead. He was released from the hospital the next day with only minor scratches and a citation for drunk driving." I struggle to hold back the tears welling inside from anger, or maybe hate.

"Do you have any idea what it's like to one minute be a happy family and the next to have no family? In the middle of the night, a couple of policemen and a social worker came knocking on our door. They got everyone out of bed and told us we would never see our mother and father again.

"Then they took me and my brothers, Rick, and Tom to the Juvenile Detention Center because we were minors. A drunk driver killed our parents, and we had to go to jail. We stayed there for two days, and then we were put in a foster home, so someone could take care of us." Now I can't keep the tremor and crack out of my voice.

"My eldest brother Randy was away at school when it happened. As soon as he got back to town, he started working to pull our family back together. We were all able to come back home, but it took a month for him to convince the welfare department and the judge we could function as a family. Even then it wasn't final. We were put in Randle's custody, but we were on probation. If anyone of us had any problem of any kind coming to the attention of the social worker or the court, our family would be dissolved, and we three minors would be wards of the court in permanent foster care."

"We fought hard to be together and finally won. But once we were all back in the house, we wondered what we had. What's a family without parents? How do you live without a mom and dad? Somehow, we got by." I can't mask the seething anger in my voice.

"Three older brothers could never replace a mom and dad. I know they did their best. I love them to pieces, but it's just not the same. It's just not fair. That drunk driver spent a month in jail. He went to an alcohol recovery center for a month, and the judge took away his license for a year. Now, everything's fine in his life. We're the ones who paid and are still paying, not him."

"The law won't let a person with epilepsy drive unless his physician certifies his seizures are under control with medication. If the law had real penalties for people who drink and drive, my parents might be alive today."

My comments end about thirty seconds before the bell rings. I look into the shocked faces of my classmates who don't know what to say. They all know I live with my brothers, but until this moment I have never talked about it publicly. The bell rings and gives a giant escape from the tension which has built to a peak. I try to catch Pam's eyes to see what effect the debate has had, but Pam's gaze never leaves the floor as she walks out the door. There were no points scored in this "friendly discussion", but I know I'm the undisputed winner.

I may have won the debate this morning, but I lost more than I gained. For the sake of proving a point and putting Pam down, I opened myself up to total public display. I had no idea what I shared would become a flash point topic inflaming the whole school. The problem is I didn't think. Now I stand in the pity-poor Terry spotlight. It was the dumbest thing I could have done.

This has been the worst school day of my life, but it's not over yet. I wish Paul would get here so we can get his math tutoring over with. The plus about meeting in this glassed-in library cubicle is it blocks out all the, "I'm so sorry about your parents," comments I've been bombarded with all day. Paul's the last person I want to feel sorry for me. I guess I'll soon hear his comments; I see he's now working his way through the study tables in the library.

He flashes me his mischievous grin as he comes through the door, "Hi

Terry, I hardly expected to find you still at school. You dropped quite a bombshell on your American Problems class this morning."

"I did it to prove a point. I just didn't expect the backlash it would bring."

"Oh Terry, I hardly think people feeling sorry for you and caring about you is a backlash. And just what point were you trying to prove?"

I can't tell him my real goal was to put Pam down, so I jump to my second objective. "Paul, I don't want people to feel sorry for me. I want them to dislike drunk drivers as much as I do. I hate that drunken imbecile! He killed my parents and ruined my life!"

"I sure wish my life was ruined like yours." I give him a totally surprised look. "You are one of the smartest, if not the smartest student in this school. Look at you! You're a junior in the senior AP Calculus class, and you ace out every student in there. You are a concert pianist. You have the looks of a fashion model or Miss. America, and you are one of the top tennis players in the state."

Before I can even thank him for his compliments, my mind pushes my anger up again and flashes back to the state tennis championships. "Not the top tennis player. That honor belongs to Miss. Pamela Fletcher."

Paul hesitates, "Oh yes, Pam, your arch-nemesis. If you ever got to know her, you would find you two are more alike than you could ever imagine. You both have a demon you nurse and are both filled with an insatiable thirst for excellence. If you did take on a project together, nothing on this earth would stand in your way."

Not liking where this conversation is going, I completely change directions. "Are you ready to tackle your math this afternoon? This is our last session before the AP exam tomorrow."

We work hard at calculations until Paul is confident that he understands the new assignment we were given today. We then review his questions for the AP test. He finally leans back and smiles at me.

"I think I'm ready—" He continues peering deep into my eyes, "Terry, I'll never be able to repay you for all the tutoring time you've freely given me. How about letting me take you to dinner tonight?"

"I love helping you, Paul. You don't owe me anything. Besides, it helps me review and cements the concepts in my brain. Tom has probably already started dinner. I need to give him a heads-up if I'm not going to be there. I'll take a rain check for another time, though."

"Okay, rain check it is. How about a ride to your house?"

"I'll take you up on the ride."

CHAPTER 3

I walk into my bedroom when I get home and drop my huge pile of books on the desk. I look at the bed considering its possibilities. I didn't have time to make it before school, so it isn't inviting. My indecision ends quickly, as I throw up the covers and sprawl out across the bedspread. I need a few minutes to ponder this day and organize what's left of it.

I can't believe Paul asked me out to dinner. It's a dream come true. I really like him; he is such a mature no-nonsense guy. If my anger weren't almost to a non-controllable point, I would have gone with him. I am embarrassed I paraded my disdain for Pam in front of him. It was like my anger had power over me instead of me dictating it.

I look at the stack of books knowing I have mega homework in every class. I don't know if all the time I put into the debate was worth it or not, and everything's due. This is the last week before finals, and I spent so much time on that dumb assignment. I'm behind in every class. It'll take hours tonight to get caught up.

My gaze shifts from the books to the ceiling, and my mind travels back to the debate. Was it worth it? I feel good my team came out on top. I feel especially good I scored a victory over Pam, but it's not a victory I'm proud of. I have never talked to the kids at school, not even to my best friends, about the accident. I didn't want anyone to feel sorry for me. Now I have revealed my tragedy to get even and be number one. It may have put Pam down, but I'm still frustrated and angry at the same time, and I don't feel on top at all.

My mind moves back to the homework. I've got to get busy, or I'll never keep my 4.0 GPA. How can I ever concentrate on schoolwork when everything else nags at my mind for attention? With my agitation growing, I leap up off the bed and find myself in front of my dressing mirror talking out loud,

"Two weeks and school is out. Two more weeks, and I'm at camp, no homework, no tests, no pressure. I can't wait. Oh, how I wish I were singing around a campfire tonight."

Pulled by an unseen force, I rush out of my room, down the hall, and turn right into the large living room instead of left into the kitchen where Tom is fixing dinner. My steps make a straight line for my baby grand piano. My fingers begin playing before I can even decide what to play. I know I must play something hard, fast, and loud. I attack Beethoven's "Sonata Pathetique" with more energy than I have ever played it.

I notice Tom has come in from the kitchen and is leaning against the doorway. When I finish the "Pathetique", he interjects a comment before I can go on to another piece. "You sound ready for your scholarship recital a whole year early. Did you have a bad day at school?"

I lightly finger the keys as I answer without looking up. "It was okay."

"You always take out your frustrations on those black and whites. I haven't heard you play like that for at least a year. What happened today? Anything to do with the friendly debate?"

I still watch the keys and play softly as I speak. "The debate went like I thought it would. I just don't feel like I imagined I would. I'll be okay; I just need to play for a while."

I know when I am down, the piano is my best friend. I can communicate all my feelings without saying a word. As I pour all my emotions into the keyboard, it melts away my frustrations and gives me peace. I am thankful this is one of my rewards for the uncounted hours of learning how to play.

As music fills the air again, Tom heads back to the kitchen. He seems to be talking to the air and the music as he makes one more comment. "Dinner will be ready in about an hour. I've got some exciting news to tell you."

Over the next hour, my music changes from explosive energy as I attack Beethoven and Brahms to a soft gentle touch as I cradled "Jessica's Theme" from *The Man From Snowy River*. In between, I play "Clair de Lune", "Rhapsody in Blue," and my all-time favorite "You Raise Me Up." My mind relaxes, as I move from music that takes all my physical energies to play, to music that makes me feel good.

Feeling more on top of life than I have in over a week, I open my music books to the pieces I am learning for the scholarship tryouts. I don't feel in a serious learning mood, so I just started playing through the list. I don't stop to make corrections. I just play. I start with Bach's *Fantasia in C Minor*, go next to Brahms' *Hungarian Dance #5*, struggle through Tchaikovsky's *Andante Cantabile*, and am just beginning Chopin's *Minute Waltz* when Tom's voice breaks my concentration.

When I am playing, I have no concept of time. I'm surprised when I realize Tom is calling me to dinner. I want to play more but know I had better stop, eat, and attack my daunting pile of homework.

Playing mostly with my food, I eat little. I only gave one-word answers when Tom tries to engage me in conversation. About halfway through the meal, I remember Tom's comment and come out of my trance. I turned my full attention to Tom.

"What's this exciting news?"

"You amaze me at times, sis; I didn't think you heard a word I said. I want to show you more than tell you—don't move!" Without finishing the bite on his fork, Tom rushes out of the room and returns with his arms full of boxes. "Happy school's out."

"Tom, what's all this?"

"Open the boxes and see. Open the biggest one first."

I open the largest box and gently lift out a skirt and top. They are soft to the touch, and the colors are pink and brown casually melted and swirled together. I look at Tom with tears in my eyes and no ability to speak.

With a hint of tears in his eyes, Tom rescues me, "Since you're at the end of your junior year, I thought it was time you finally went to your first dance. I know the School's Out Dance is this Friday, and I want you to go. Open the other boxes." I slowly open the next box and hold up a soft sweater that matches the skirt and blouse. The next box contains white sandals to complete the outfit. The last little box yields simple make-up and a necklace. I can tell by his voice Tom is as excited as I am when he says, "Well, what are you waiting for? Go try them on." I snatch up my treasures to leave, as Tom continues, "The clerk and I guessed at your sizes. If anything doesn't fit, she said to bring it back, and you can exchange it." Again, he seems to be talking to the air. I am down the hall and almost into my room by the time he finishes.

I lay the boxes side by side on the bed and stare at their contents. It has been years since I have had a new outfit. There are plenty of hand-me-down shirts and jeans from three older brothers but no skirts or dresses. This is like being awake in a dream I've dreamt so many times. I'm elated that he picked out simple yet stylish clothes. I loathe ruffly things; I touch the sweater to make sure it isn't a dream. I'm also glad he chose sandals. Heels make me too tall, and I move awkwardly in them. Tom's voice breaks through my daydream from the kitchen,

"Are you dressed yet?"

In five minutes, I have everything on, except for the make-up, and am on my way back down the hall to the kitchen.

Tom gives a loud wolf whistle when I float through the door. "Wow, I knew I had a cute sister, but when you put chic clothes on her, I'm not sure it's safe for her to go to the dance."

"Oh, Tom! Don't be silly."

"I'm not exaggerating one bit. Terry, you're prettier than any girls I've seen at the high school or the college for that matter."

"Tom, you haven't even been at the high school for three years."

"Girls don't change, and I say you're the cutest of all."

"Thanks, Tom."

My smiling face changes to one of concern. I love the clothes, but I am beginning to feel the nagging reality of our situation. "Where did you get the money for all this, anyway?"

"Terry, you've been a super good sport about not having money and going without. I know you've turned down dates because you don't have anything to wear. I just want you to enjoy a dance before you're out of high school and the chance is gone."

"Tom, you still didn't answer my question. Where did you get the money? Did you rob a bank?"

Tom laughs as he answers, "No, I didn't rob any bank. This last semester at school has been light, so my boss let me work some extra hours here and there and on Saturdays. If we won't let you work, the least I can do is help you get a few things you need. The clerk sure knew what would look good on you."

I am satisfied with his answer and turn my attention back to the clothes. "How did you pick things out? Everything fits perfectly, even the shoes."

"I just went into this clothing store and said I need a sharp outfit for the cutest girl in town."

"Tom, you did not."

"Yes, I did. Then the sales lady asked me what this cute girl looked like. I told her you were 5'10" and weighed about 130 lbs. You had short black curly hair and great big brown eyes, and I showed her a picture of you. I took a pair of your tennis shoes with me to get the right shoe size."

I whirl around the kitchen and then give Tom a big hug. "Thank you, Tom. You'll never know what this means to me. Maybe someone will even ask me to dance, and I can try out all those dancing lessons you've been giving me for years." I float down the hall as I say, "Right now I had better dance to my homework, or I'll—"

"Terry," Tom cuts my sentence short. "There is something else I have wanted to talk to you about." I stop and whirl around but say nothing. I brace myself for what I can guess is coming. "Why can't I pin you down for a family prayer anymore? If you won't pray with me, I'll bet you aren't having any personal prayers either. It would help calm the anger inside before it eats you alive. What's—"

"Tom, please don't ruin this night!" I half yell and cry while turning and running for my room. Tom shakes his head and turns back into the kitchen. Reaching the safety of my door, I fling myself on my bed again amidst all the empty boxes. Facedown on my pillow with closed eyes and hot burning tears, I carry on my conversation in my head. I'm not angry; I'm tired of being second. And prayer is a total joke! I usually play the part well; even saying all the right words. It's just getting harder and harder to pretend. If there is a God, He doesn't listen in this house. In case Tom doesn't remember, we had a family prayer before mom and dad left the night they were killed. Rick prayed for their safe return. What an answer we got! If there is a God, He expects us to be completely on our own, and that's what I'm going to do. I'm going to be somebody; I'm going to get a music scholarship; I'm going to college; I'm going to be a concert pianist, and I'm going to do it on my own. With that resolve, I push myself up off the bed and plop into the chair at my desk. At about 1:00 am, I close my last book and fall back into bed.

Throughout the rest of the week, my mind returns regularly to the outfit hanging in my closet. I also think of all the times my friends have tried to get me to go to the stag dances. I gave them a different excuse each time, but I'm sure they've decided I don't know how to dance. Each of my brothers has taught me a little, but Tom has spent the most time with me. I think of the many hours we have been in the living room dancing to all kinds of music. With something to wear, now there is only one obstacle left. When I get there, will someone ask me to dance?

Friday night finally comes. At 7 p.m. sharp, I appear in the living room for my final inspection. As I walk through the doorway, the room fills with claps, shouts, and wolf whistles. I now stand in front of three brothers instead of one. When the noise mellows, I stand tall, put my hands on my hips, and say, "Don't tell me you two came home from your schools this weekend just to watch me get ready for some little dance."

Again come the claps, whistles, and shouts from all three brothers. When their noise dies down, my oldest brother, Randy says, "Tom said this is something we shouldn't miss. He was right. You are the most gorgeous girl in town. It's a good thing you don't wear clothes like these all the time. You'd have so many dates, you'd never do homework. What do you think guys? Should we all go to the dance and chaperon our not-so-little sister?" This brings another round of laughter.

I start to frown, not knowing if my brothers are honestly considering attending the dance. Tom seems to sense my fears and interrupts to save the moment. Holding out his hand, he says, "Here are the keys to my car. There should be enough wheels around here tonight to take me to any place I might need to go. You can stop for a Coke after the dance if you like, but please come straight home after that. We'll all be waiting up for you."

With that, I take the keys, and he walks me out to his car. I'm silent until we get to the driver's door. When Tom opens it, I turned to talk, but Tom takes the words out of my mouth. "Terry, don't worry about tonight. We've all been to plenty of these dances. We know you might get asked to dance every dance, or you might not get asked to dance once. We just want you to know we're proud of you, no matter what. It has nothing to do with how the dance turns out. Now go! Be yourself, and you'll have a good time."

"Thanks, Tom. You guys are great! Don't have too much fun without me."

Tom gives me a big smile and a wink as he closes me into his car.

I take a big breath and open the door to the school gym where the dance is being held. I am amazed at the transformation which has taken place. The ceiling has been lowered with a blanket of crepe paper and balloons. The walls have mural-like posters of every summer activity you could think of. The lights are dimmed, and contemporary dance music fills the air. I don't have long to take in the new atmosphere, however. A group of my girlfriends spot me then engulf me. Comments seem to come from everyone at once. Joan asks, "How come you didn't tell us you were coming to the dance? We'd have picked you up."

Hillary comments from my left side, "Hey, you look sharp. When did you get your new clothes?"

"I didn't think you ever came to dances." Jean's voice comes at me from the right.

Another voice I don't recognize calls out, "How did you get here?"

I feel as if I am in a whirlwind until Jed breaks into our group and saves me from answering any questions. "Terry, would you like to dance?"

The group falls silent almost instantly to see what my answer will be.

I know they think I can't dance, and they are waiting to see what I will say. "Sure, Jed, I'd love to; that's what I'm here for."

Linking my arm through his, I follow him out into the middle of the floor. The eyes of my entire group of friends and those of many others throughout the gym follow me as the music starts again. I easily follow all the steps Jed wants to try. I know that I am somewhat on trial and silently say, Thank you Tom for all those hours of dancing lessons.

I dance two dances with Jed and am making my way back to my group of friends when Blake catches me by the arm. "Terry, it's neat to see you here. Come and dance with me."

The first hour of the dance is about the same. I just get through dancing with one guy and another asks me before I can get back to my group. The dancing is easy and fun. I find talking to guys is as easy as dancing. I have made friends with most of the boys in my classes over the years and have always found it easy to talk to them. Since I have never been to a dance, I was afraid it might be different here. I discover it's just as easy to talk to them on the dance floor as it is in the classroom; maybe easier, the teacher isn't watching.

After one especially fast dance, I make my way to the drinking fountain. When the boy in front of me finishes his drink and turns around, to my surprise it is someone I knew quite well, "Hi Paul."

"Hi Terry, I didn't know you were here."

"I snuck in when you weren't looking. How did you do on the AP calculus test?"

"Thanks to you, I aced it. I don't even need to ask how you did."

When I finish my drink, Paul puts his arm behind my back while saying, "Come dance with me." He maneuvers me onto the dance floor. Feeling a new excitement, I let myself be guided into our first dance, then the next, and the next.

We have spent time together almost every school day. During the last month of our tutoring sessions, we found it easier and easier to talk about everything that interests us, but we still made math come first. Tonight, there is no math, and it is so pleasant to be with him. He holds me just a little closer and talks just a little more freely than any of my other dance partners had. I begin to feel as if this could be an incredibly special evening.

After we have danced for about a half-hour, Paul says, "Terry, you are a phenomenal dancer. I claim you to be my partner for the rest of the evening. Let's find a place to sit a few out, then I'll show you off some more."

We are just moving off the dance floor when someone steps in front of us blocking our way. "Hi, Paul! Hi Terry! Looks like a fun dance."

To my shock, amazement, and horror, Pam is standing in front of us. All I can utter is, "Hi Pam."

Paul picks up the conversation, "Hi, Pam. See you got back earlier from your trip than you thought. It's a good dance. Almost everyone's here."

Pam seems quite disgusted as she directs her comments to Paul. "I'd like the chance to see if it's fun. Paul, I need to talk to you outside."

Paul turns to me, "Terry thanks for the dances. It's sure good to see you here—I remember I still owe you a dinner." With that comment, he follows Pam to the door and out.

I'm now in total shock. How could I feel on cloud nine one minute and squashed flat by a steam roller the next? I want to cry right here on the spot. I didn't know Paul was going with anyone, least of all Pam. The only time he ever mentioned her name was after the debate when he said we were both nursing demons, whatever that meant.

I am trying to decide if I can make a fifty-yard dash out the door to the car when Jed taps me on the shoulder, "Terry, would you like to dance again? I like dancing with you; you make me look good."

I force a smile and a nod as I investigate his eager face.

I am glad the dance is fast, so we don't need to talk much. The fast steps ease my pain a little and trying to be pleasant for Jed keeps me from falling apart. I try three more dances with three different partners, but the excitement for the night is gone.

Before anyone else can ask me to dance again, I make a beeline for the water fountain. After drinking, I turn and escape through the side door. I drive slowly and take the longest way home planning how to convince my brothers the dance was great when all I feel is I came in second again.

CHAPTER 4

Right now, I'm on a bus, but not the one that will deliver me to Camp. This one is taking me to the Augustine University Campus for the composition competition awards night. Four months ago, I saw a notice in the newspaper announcing a composition contest sponsored by the Music Department of the University. I had been having this melody claim my attention more than I wanted, so I decided to turn it into a sonata and enter the contest. It took me right up to the deadline to finish because all the transcription had to be done by hand. I don't have access to a recording keyboard. Maybe someday… in my dreams.

When I told Tom I wanted to do this, he was enthusiastic and encouraged me in every way he could. He had to work late tonight, so we arranged to meet at the university. I'm excited to see how I compare with anyone who's composing. When I walk into the Lilian Masters Auditorium, it takes my breath away. I haven't been here since my mom's last concert before the accident.

There must be a lot of want-to-be composers because the auditorium is almost full. The seats are occupied by people of all ages. It's hard to tell which ones are composers and which are their supporters. Tom slips into the seat I saved for him just as the program begins. I learn the evening has been sponsored by a group of senior piano majors as their composition project. They have picked five compositions to award cash prizes to, and two honorable mentions to be given certificates. They begin with honorable mentions and work their way to first place. They announce the person and their piece, then the composer comes onto the stage to perform their number and receive their award.

I am disappointed in the level of the compositions. Most of the music they are playing I was composing in kindergarten. It does get a little more advanced as the program moves toward first place, but not much. When the top composer is announced, I'm surprised, shocked, and angry it's not me. Tom glances at me with a look of dismay. I just shake my head and whisper, "Maybe they didn't get my composition in the mail before the deadline. We'll ask after everyone leaves.

The last person is walking out the door as Tom and I are walking across the stage to the senior composition committee. One of them turns to look at us, "Yes, can we help you?"

"My name is Terry Masters, and I want to know if you didn't receive my composition, 'Odyssey'?"

"Oh yes, we received it. I can't believe you would even show your face here." I am stunned. She goes on, "We disqualified it for blatant plagiarism. You copied some obscure classical composer and turned it in as your own."

Now my brain is beginning to work on overdrive, "Plagiarism! I want you to know every note in that piece is my creation. It's handwritten because I don't have access to a recording printer. Which composer do you think I copied? You can't claim plagiarism unless you can show what I've copied."

An older man who looks somewhat familiar joins our group. "What seems to be the problem here?"

"This girl turned in a composition that has obviously been plagiarized. She is trying to convince us she wrote it." She holds up the manuscript, "This is prodigy music, she's way too young to compose anything like this."

Now I'm on fire, "So are you telling me everything Beethoven claimed to write before he was twenty was plagiarized? You know every composer has a theme or style that's recognizable. You tell me one composer this even comes close to." The older man is now looking carefully through my composition. "I'll even play it for you, and you can tell me which composer you think I copied."

Another of the committee members sarcastically says, "Now that's a real joke. If we can't play it, you couldn't even attempt it. This is all a waste of time. The 'Odyssey' has been disqualified."

"Oh, I get it now. You can't play it so that disqualifies me. If you can't prove plagiarism, that means you have slandered me."

I am ready to fight when the older man speaks, "Miss. Masters this is quite a piece you've written. Let me have a week to allow this committee to search for any evidence of plagiarism. When they find none, you will receive a full apology from them and the University along with the grand prize money for this competition. I'm sorry for the lack of research on their part."

He's drenched most of my fire, but I will have the last word, "You're gits. You don't have the foggiest notion of what the real piano world is like." Tom and I make a hasty retreat.

I ask while Tom's driving, "Do you know who the older man was? He seemed to be the authority over those gits."

"I don't know who he is, but I think he was a teacher when mom taught here. Tell you what I do know, he's positive you wrote 'Odyssey'." I agree with Tom on that.

Three days later I receive a special delivery letter from Augustine University. Inside are all the apologies plus a certified check for double the first-place prize money. He did make it a grand prize, whoever he is.

I'm sitting at the piano hitting random keys not playing anything trying to decide if my experience with the composition contest was good or poor. It was obvious my music was over the heads of the seniors, and they didn't know what to do with it. Their faculty advisor seemed to like what he saw. So where am I?

To answer that question my cell phone rings. The caller ID says it's

Paul Young. Wonder what he's up to, "Hi Paul, this is Terry."

"Hope I'm not calling you too late."

"No, still wide awake having a philosophical debate with myself. What's up?"

"Are you kind of a wilderness woman?" Now I'm mystified.

"I guess I could wear that title. What are you thinking?"

"I know I owe you a dinner, but I'm wondering if I could trade for a hike up the canyon to the hot pots? My friends tell me it's a cool place. Not tomorrow, but maybe the following day. I would like to do something with you before you leave for camp."

Now he has my interest, "I would love to do that. I'll pack us lunch and we can have a steak fry by the stream. What time do you want to leave?" I can't believe this is happening.

"I'll pick you up at about 6 am. We will avoid the heat and the crowd. Thanks, Terry, I'm looking forward to a fantastic day. The weather's supposed to be clear and warm. See you at six." Did he mean our date or the weather would be fantastic? Whatever he meant, I'm excited to have a real date with Paul…I like him a lot.

He pulls into the driveway at 6:00 am sharp. I'm sitting on the porch in my wilderness woman hiking clothes and boots. I hope he's not expecting short shorts and a halter top. I breathe a sigh of relief when he steps from his truck in long pants, a long-sleeved shirt, and hiking boots. We've never talked about either of our outdoor experiences. This day ought to be very interesting.

Hiking up the trail to the hot springs I casually ask him if he's an outdoor man. He says, "My family doesn't like outdoor or nature activities at all. My uncle is an avid outdoorsman, and I love to tag along with him when I can. I've spent time with him hiking, backpacking, kayaking, and hunting most summers since I was eight. I remembered you saying something about a camping trip with your parents, so I thought you might be up for a hike."

"I'm up for a hike anytime. I love doing anything in nature." I get him to tell me about some of his adventures with his uncle, and I can see we share the same enthusiasm for outdoor living."

It seems like we have just started hiking when we round a bend and the hot springs come into view. When we stop on the trail above the springs, his expression changes to one of concern. I'm about to ask him what the problem is when I can hear the group that's been following us for some time catching up to us. I'm extremely disappointed when a senior boy, whom I call Jerk Jake in my mind, comes into view with a skimpily dressed girl and another couple dressed as sparsely.

When he spots Paul, he laughs and sarcastically mocks, "Goody-boy Paul, I never thought I'd see you at the hot springs, especially with the most beautiful but untouchable Terry Masters. What are you waiting for, get them clothes off." He and his friends start shedding what few clothes they have on. Paul turns red and is speechless.

Jake notices his hesitation, "Come on Paul. This is what these hot springs are used for. We've had as many as twenty couples in this little pond at one time. There's a lot of sharing going on then. If you'll hold Terry down, we'll give her a little something that will take away all her inhibitions. Nothing's off-limits here." They are now all in the water, and Paul is still stunned.

But I'm not, "No thanks Jerk, I mean Jake. We just stopped to look at the springs. Our destination is much further up the trail. There's some beautiful scenery up there, and we've brought our cameras to capture it. When we leave this canyon, we'll still be temple worthy."

"Yaa yaa, all that morality stuff is way overrated. You have fun and excitement with the taboos when you're young and repent when the time comes. That way you get the best of both worlds. Sorry, you prudes are going to miss all the fun."

I take hold of Paul's hand and pull him up the trail. We walk hand in hand for at least a half-mile until I'm sure we're well out of hearing range of the springs. I stop and turn to face Paul standing about twelve inches from his face, "Paul…

I can't get out more words when he sobs, "Terry, I am so embarrassed. I had no idea anything like that happens up here. Please forgive me. I would never subject you to anything like that. I would never participate in something so obscene." Tears of anguish are still rolling down his cheeks as he stares at the ground.

I put my hands on his cheeks and lift his head to look into his eyes, "Paul Young, with complete honesty, I want you to tell me why you brought me to the hot springs with you. We're good enough friends that you can level with me."

He squeezes his eyes shut and takes a deep breath. Opening his eyes he starts, "Terry, I like you. I like you a lot. Spending time with you every day after school has shown me what a cool down-to-earth person with fabulous abilities you are. You're not full of yourself, you're just good. I've wanted to date you for a long time. I just didn't know if you would consider going out with someone who's not as smart as you." He pauses hunting for words, "After the dance, I decided I was going to give dating a try. You felt so good in my arms.

"I ask my friends to tell me where the most romantic place in the mountains is. Separately, three of them said the hot springs were at the top of their list. I've never been here, so I took their word for it. Romance in my mind is not the same as a sex orgy. My greatest hope was to get away with kissing you if you didn't object. I am so sorry I placed you in such a compromised position."

I'm still holding his head to look into his eyes, "Paul, you didn't compromise me. Jake and his crowd are obscene, rude slobs. They try to squish everything good to justify their behaviors…I want you to know you are the only guy I have wished would ask me out this entire year. You also need to know I have been to the hot springs before." His mouth gapes open in shock, "When I was ten years old…My family camped further up the canyon, and we all came down to swim in the warm water. We were all wearing our swimming suits. It can be a fun place to swim and play in the water…With you here, I think almost any place in this canyon has a romantic air." The look of horror in his eyes is changing to one of excitement. My heart begins to race, and I do something I've never done before but feels so natural. I slip my hands behind his neck, pull his head forward and plant a kiss on his lips. It was meant to be a quick kiss, but his arms wrap around me, and it becomes a long lingering kiss that starts a fire in my whole being. I've kissed boys before, but nothing like this has ever happened.

When we finally come up for air, neither of us knows what to say. I grab his hand again, "Come on, I've got some places I want to show you, and we've got a lunch to cook."

About a mile further up the trail, we come to a stream that has a fire circle next to it. Twenty feet from the stream the trees open where a cliff drops straight down for 2,000 feet. The vista which opens shows a panorama extending for miles. Paul puts his arm around my waist, "Oh Terry, this is the most beautiful spot I have ever seen. This gives me goosebumps all over. You can almost see eternity here. A camera could never do this justice. Thank you." He squeezes me closer to him, and I feel warm all over.

My stomach is telling me the view time is over. I move back into the trees and begin gathering downed wood to start the fire. I notice a dead log that would be perfect to sit on by the fire. I ask Paul if he would drag it over. He easily bends over, picks it up, and carries it to the fire ring. He has muscles to go with his looks. He seems impressed I start the fire with my flint and steel and hand him a steak threaded on a green willow to cook. We enjoy the meal laughing and teasing about school, the hot springs, and life ahead. I think I could learn to love him

He lays a blanket on the grass, and I lay down for my favorite game of finding animals and objects in the clouds. The time flies quickly, and I realize we need to be heading back if we don't want to go down the trail in the dark.

I am about ready to suggest we start when I find myself looking into Paul's face inches from mine. I think I should object to what's coming, but I don't want to. This kiss lasts longer and is more intense than the first one. When we part, I sit up quickly, I have a clear understanding of one thing. "Paul, we can never do that again unless we're married. We're too young to marry. You need to go on your mission in August, and I need to finish school that I haven't even started. Besides, we are going to leave this canyon still temple-worthy."

"No girl has ever made me feel this way before. I love you. Say the word Terry, and I'll stay home from my mission."

"You know we can't. Let's get on the trail." I instantly load my backpack and hand the blanket to Paul.

Then I have a thought, "Those friends of yours who sent you to the hot springs. I know you'd like to kill them, but I have a better punishment. When they ask you how your date was, tell them you had the most exciting, beautiful day of your life. It won't be a lie, at least for me it won't. When they ask what you did, tell them that's private between you and me. Never tell them another thing, ever. It'll drive them crazy. What will be even better is that Jerk Jake will tell everyone he saw us at the hot springs."

"Terry, I knew you were a genius."

For our return trip, we're back in our friend mode and enjoy a companionable conversation. When we get to my house it's almost dark outside. The house windows are lit, but the porch light is off. Paul walks me to the door holding my hand. When we stop, we both stare hard at each other. I raise on my toes and give him a peck on the cheek. My last words are, "Have fun in Europe on your graduation trip." I walk in and close the door leaning back against it wondering if I just shut the door on a fabulous future.

I'm brought back to the present by Tom's voice, "Terry, is that you?"

"It's me."

"I'm in the front room." I know that's an invitation to talk. I might as well get it over with. I walk in and flop into a stuffed chair across the coffee table from him.

He doesn't waste any time, "How was your all-day date with Paul?"

I decide to use my own words, "It was the most exciting, beautiful day of my entire life."

He looks at me with his twinkling eyes and almost a smirk on his face, "You kissed him, didn't you? And he kissed you back even harder with more passion. Your whole being was lit on fire. He told you he loved you and wanted to marry you. He would even stay home from his mission. You were more important. My big question is what did you tell him?"

I am so shocked, I would have fallen out of this chair if it didn't have arms, "Tom how do you know all that? I'm positive you weren't there. Did you plant a listening device on me?" I'm speechless.

"No Terry, there's no listening bug on you, and I've been at work all day. Let me tell you about the most exciting, beautiful day of my life to this point...But first I need to share a conversation dad and I once had."

"When I was at a point where kissing girls was my overarching goal, we had one of his talks. He told me about the hormone changes in my body that were attracting me to girls. He said it was in preparation for finding a mate. He was very emphatic that just any mate would not do. Besides looking for romance, I needed to be looking for someone who would be my best friend for time and eternity. We needed to grow a friendship to find out if we even liked being with each other. A lifetime was a long time and eternity was even longer.

"Once the friendship was established, I could check out the hormones with a kiss. If it felt like I was kissing my sister, this was probably not the right woman to spend eternity with. After my mission, I needed to look for an eternal friend and then stop at the temple sealing room before I gave all my hormones full sway.

"Now, about my exciting, beautiful day. I don't know if you remember Gail or not. We met just before I receive my mission call. She was the neatest girl I had ever gone with. We enjoyed the same things, she laughed at my dumb jokes, and she was kind to everyone, not just me. She always made me feel like a king. One day I decided to take her on a hike up the canyon to add a little romance to our relationship. About halfway up the trail, I couldn't wait any longer and I kissed her. She kissed me back in a way I had never been kissed before, I was on fire. Now I knew what dad was talking about. We were both a little embarrassed and didn't say much the rest of the way up to the lookout. We ate our lunch by the stream, and we looked for images in the clouds while lying on the ground. I thought all my feelings were under control, and she must have thought the same thing. We turned to look into each other's eyes at the same time. Instantly we were locked in each other's arms in a much more passionate kiss."

"When we finally broke apart, I said, "Gail, I love you with all my heart. Will you marry me? I don't need to go on a mission; I've found the right one."

"She broke our embrace and sat straight up, 'Tom we're too young to get married. I have deep feelings for you, but we would never forgive ourselves if you didn't go on your mission. Your parents would turn over in their graves. Besides, I want to leave this canyon still temple-worthy, and I want to marry a returned missionary.' With that, she packed us up, led me down the canyon, and I went on my mission."

"I will never forget her…She was married when I got back. But I will always be thankful for what she kept us from. She also taught me what I want my eternal companion to be like, and I will look until I find her—Now what did you say to Paul?"

I can't believe what he just told me, "Oh Tom, we must be brother and sister. You couldn't have painted my day more accurately than you explained yours, right down to the kiss on the trail, to the finding objects in the clouds lying on a blanket, to the last wondrous kiss. The only thing you didn't have in your day was Jerk Jake skinny dipping with his gang in the hot springs as we passed by."

"The hot springs always were unpredictable for orgies. What did you tell Paul? Am I getting ready for a wedding?"

"Of course, we're not getting married. Ditto for Gail's words. We both came out of the canyon still temple-worthy, and Paul will go on his mission in August."

Tom gets out of his chair and comes toward me with his arms outstretched for a hug. I stand to meet him. With his arms wrapped around me, he whispers, "I'm so proud of you Terry. One day Paul will thank you, but not until after his mission."

I look up into Tom's face with a smile, "But it was a romantically exciting, beautiful day."

"It was, wasn't it!" he says with gleaming eyes.

CHAPTER 5

I had no idea I would be traveling by plane to my last year of camp at Lightning Mountain. For being a first-time flier, I think I've done well so far. I managed to check my luggage with Tom's help, find the gate after clearing security, and I'm now seated in a window seat which I'm hoping is the seat designated on my ticket.

The letter I got from Mrs. Scott said because I am eighteen, I will not only be a junior leader but will also be considered an assistant unit leader. As such, I need to participate in the pre-camp staff orientation the week before the campers arrive. During orientation, she wants me to teach some outdoor cooking, plant identification, and maybe some climbing and repelling if anyone is interested.

I was looking forward to riding on one of the charter buses with some of the other junior leaders and getting to know the campers. It was always a fun time to sing and get hyped up for camp. I'm looking out the tiny window when I feel a presence in the aisle. My stomach sinks and a wave of nausea floods over me as I watch Pam look at her ticket, look at the seat numbers, and look at me. She takes a deep breath, stows her carry-on in the overhead compartment, and slips into the seat beside me. I turn my head back to look out the window. What a nightmare this is going to be. She stands back up to pull a book out of her carry-on. Without speaking a word, she dives into the middle of her book. The only defense I have is to close my eyes and pretend to sleep.

I settle back in my seat closing my eyes; my mind races in five directions at once. All the events of the past few months prance into my consciousness, but none stay long enough to be thought about in any detail. All the finals and the hours of study flash by in my mind. The horrible tennis match soars in and out. I see piles of homework, hours of piano practicing, and hours of tennis workouts. The debate slips in, the unfinished conversation with Tom about prayer joins the parade, and then all the pain of the accident so many years ago stabs at me for an instant. The study hours with Paul appear, and then they dance away. I relive for a moment the all-night party with my girlfriends we put together on the last night of school. I smile as I think of all the silly games we played. Then there was the all-day hike with Paul. My mind lingers on the feelings aroused that day. I feel anger as I wonder if Pam likes him, but I need to let that go. I sent him away to go on a mission, and I have no claim on him. My mind then skips to packing for camp, and I begin to relax.

Lightening Mountain Camp has been a part of me as far back as I can remember. My mom had been on the staff before marrying, and it was just a fact of life I would become a camper as soon as I was old enough. I think of my first summer at camp. I can still recall every detail. I had been scared and excited all at once. After four exciting summers at Lightning Mountain, I figured my camping days were through when my mom and dad were killed. But because of the scholarships my parents had furnished for many deserving girls each summer, the board of directors decided to scholarship me. If I worked hard and wanted to come, I could return to camp each summer until I graduated from high school.

This is the summer I have looked forward to for years, and now it is here—my last summer as a camper, and yet I won't be a camper. This summer I was to be a junior leader, but I don't quite understand my dual position as an assistant unit leader too. I'm assigned to a unit and will work with the unit leaders to carry out the program. I get to use all the staff facilities and attend all the staff meetings and parties. If I do a good job, I know I will probably be hired on staff for next summer after I graduate. I'm not worried about next summer, however. This is the summer I have been waiting for, and I'm going to enjoy every minute of it.

I feel excited all over as I think about my summer assignment. I am going to be an assistant leader in one of the two out-back units. These are the oldest girls in the camp. They will spend three weeks at Lightning Mountain getting ready and then be bussed out for a two-week backpacking adventure somewhere in the West. It doesn't even dampen my excitement as I think about Pam being at camp. We have been at camp together every summer for years but have always been in different units.

Camp life stays so busy we very seldom see each other, let alone compete. Pam is an assistant leader in the other out-back unit which is like another world.

My mind rushes ahead to the end of the summer as I think about the final awards night. Stacks of awards are always given out. Everyone gets awarded something, but there is only one special award. Every year the most outstanding camper is awarded the Silver Dove Award. It usually goes to a JL in one of the out-back units. Since we're still JLs, when the time comes, Pam and I will probably be back in competition again. For now, I am going to put Pam out of my mind and enjoy the summer.

Talking breaks through my unconsciousness, "Please put your seats in the upright position and stow your tray. All seatbelts must be fastened for our landing." I wake with a start. Looking out the window, I can see we are on our approach to the landing strip. This is a much smaller airport than the one we left. I wonder who will pick us up. As soon as the seatbelt sign is turned off, Pam is in the aisle retrieving her things from the overhead rack and starts toward the door. By the time I get to the aisle, there are several passengers between us. I think that was the most pleasant conversation she and I have ever had. Not a word was spoken for three hours.

I see Pam pick up her backpack and duffel from the luggage carousel and head for the exit door. Our instructions said the camp van would be waiting outside those doors to pick us up. When I make my way through the doors, Pam is handing her pack to someone in the back of the van. She then moves to get into the back seat. It's then I notice there are several staff members in the van when they cheer and clap as Pam climbs in. I'm so glad it's not just Pam and me with whomever is driving. The front door opens, and a hand reaches to pull me into shouting and cheering. I'm looking into Dixie's smiling face. I'm so excited she's my unit leader for the summer.

An hour later we pull into the huge parking area at Lightning Mountain Camp. The place looks deserted without the buses and all the campers. Mrs. Scott is there to give each one of us a hug as we empty the van. She also tells us to take our luggage to our units and be back at the lodge in two hours for dinner and our first staff meeting. Dixie, my UL leads, and Tracy, our assistant UL follows; I bring up the rear. I'm not sure what I'm called.

It's approaching 5:30 pm and I'm getting antsy, "Dixie, don't you think we should start back to the lodge? It's a thirty-minute trek."

"Terry, I have a surprise for you and Tracy. Bring your jackets, it'll be chilly when we return." Dixie heads for the lake instead of the trail. Leaving the trees, we walk onto the shore to find there's a new dock stretching into the water and two shiny new green canoes ready for travel. Dixie slides into the middle and points to the stern and the bow, "You two can do the honors tonight." This is such fun. It will cut our travel time to the lodge to ten minutes when we need to get there fast. Dixie is quick to brag, "All of the units now have staff canoes. It will save so much time. We all also have walkie-talkies for communications."

When we tie up to the dock in front of the lodge, there's a rainbow of

59

canoes. Dixie informs us, "Each unit has a different color. That way you can look at the lake and tell where the staff is." I love all these new improvements.

Two of the many long tables with benches are set and filled with staff. We seem to be the last ones to arrive. Dixie sits next to Rusty, the other out-back UL. She was my UL last summer. She is so neat. We even did some climbing and repelling together in our free activity choices. Tracy and I are the last two on the end of our bench. As soon as we are seated, Mrs. Scott welcomes us to camp telling us we'll have our meeting after we eat, otherwise, she would never get our attention. We all stand to sing grace then two runners from each table head to the serving area to pick up our food.

I'm so thrilled to be back at camp again. I love the feeling here. It's almost peaceful enough to take away my growing agitation but not quite. We waste no time eating or clearing up. Mrs. Scott moves to stand in front of the two tables. Everyone with their back to her quickly turns to face our camp director.

"Welcome, welcome to Lightning Mountain Camp for another exciting summer." She summarizes all the improvements, for which we all clap in hardy approval. She goes on, "Most of you are probably surprised to see Pam and Terry here with the regular staff. This summer they will still hold onto their junior leader status, but since they are both eighteen, and we desperately need their skills, they will also be wearing the title of assistant unit leader this summer. What is more ironic is they are both high school seniors, but if they chose to start college this fall, they would be college juniors. Terry and Pam, welcome to our staff." We are welcomed with clapping and cheering. Mrs. Scott talks for the next hour explaining the organization for the summer.

"Tomorrow morning, we will eat breakfast in the lodge, take a short nature hike with Terry, then move to unit 2 for first aid training with Pam. Lunch will be back in the lodge. At 3:00 pm, we will meet at the Lodge fire circle where Terry will teach you how to prepare dinner. Terry, have you decided what we'll cook?"

"We're going to attempt rotisserie chicken and tinfoil vegetables. Bring your fire-starting equipment and eating utensils. If you don't want to sit on the ground, you might want a folding camp chair." We're going to use the lodge fire circle because it's large enough to make four individual fires, and I can keep an eye on everyone at the same time.

Mrs. Scott takes over again. "Every unit that Terry or Pam have been in has always gotten over-the-top education in nature, cooking, and first aid. I felt it was time all of us received this training. Now it's time to expand our music education. Terry, move to the well-worn piano and see if you can make magic happen. We did have it tuned for the summer. Pam is going to teach us some new camp songs to add to our cherished favorites." On my way to the piano, my agitation begins growing stronger. I can't believe it. On my first night here, I'm assigned to work with Pam. I can't dwell on it. I'll just concentrate on the music. That usually brings me some degree of calm.

While Pam passes out sheet music, I let my fingers check out the piano from bottom to top. When I finish and turn to look at Pam for direction, I realize every eye in the room is focused on me. Maybe they don't know I play the piano. Pam asks me to play through the first round. The second time Pam sings and everyone tries to sing with her. I didn't realize what a truly beautiful voice she has. As we work, I also realize she's done her homework. She's picked out some catchy fun music along with a few pieces that teach values. We sing for almost an hour. Pam has the staff sounding link a choir and most of the music is memorized. I will give her credit for an evening well spent.

She turns to Mrs. Scott signaling the singing session is over. "Very nice Pam. I love your choice of new music. Let's sing a few of our favorite oldies. When someone calls out a song, I begin an introduction, but at the same time, I'm careful to follow Pam's directions. To keep us from singing all night Mrs. Scot stands again, "Pam, didn't you take first place in your state with a vocal solo?" Pam nods her head. "Will you sing it for us?"

"I'm not sure Terry knows the accompaniment."

I can play her song, but I'm not sure I want to help her look good. Then I think about how bad I'll look if I don't. I begin the introduction. She should have taken state; she sings with talent and feeling. The staff gives her a standing ovation which she deserves, she even has me stand to acknowledge me as her accompanist.

We begin to walk back to our seats when Mrs. Scott stops us again, "Will the two of you perform 'You Raise Me Up'?"

Pam singing my mother's favorite song is disastrous. I look at Pam and then at Mrs. Scott and know I have no choice. She sings it with more feeling and expertise than I have ever heard it performed even professionally. And I vowed I would never help her do anything again.

It's gray dawn and I'm on the trail heading to the lake. I need to check out the spot I want to take the staff on their nature hike after breakfast. The marshy area is as I remembered it, and the cattails are just right for harvesting to put in our vegetable pack for tonight.

I find a log to concentrate on my second problem, Pam. This morning my frustration or anger level is higher than it's ever been. I'm sure Pam's a direct cause, but what do I do with it? I can't give her the silent treatment. I finally decide I'll just talk to her like any other staff member when we must work together, but I'll avoid her whenever possible.

We're just cleaning up from what I would judge a successful spit-cooked and aluminum foil dinner. Everyone seems excited to have learned a new way to cook chicken and roast vegetables. The sun has just slipped beneath the horizon when I hear the first croak of a bullfrog hiding in the shallows of the lake. I know we don't have another meeting after dinner, so I jump on an idea, "Listen up everyone. If you would like, we could take all our canoes onto the lake and gig for bullfrogs. There's more than enough out there to have a good frog-leg fry. Anyone interested?" I hear quite a few people saying yes.

Then I hear another voice louder than the rest, "We have such a nice bed of coals, we could make some-mores and sing to our heart's content."

The anger in me is too near the surface, "The moon is coming up, and it's a perfect night to go after the tasty critters." I say quite forcefully.

"Well, some of us would just as soon leave your tasty friends alone."

I heatedly say, "Let's divide. Anyone who wants to learn more about survival living come with me, and the rest of you squeamish ones stay with Pam." I regret the words as soon as they're out of my mouth, but I'm too angry to take anything back. The staff pretty much divides in half, and my half is off to gig frogs.

We're about ready to eat the prizes we brought back from the lake when Rusty rushes into the kitchen and touches me on the shoulder, "Mrs. Scott wants you in her office ASAP." She then rushes out the side kitchen door. I finish eating my first frog leg wanting more but walk quickly to Scott's office. Pam and I arrive at the office door at the same time. We give each other a questioning look and Pam turns the nob to walk in.

Mrs. Scott looks anything but happy. "Just what do you two think you're doing?"

I'm shocked at her anger, "I thought it would be okay to go gigging for frogs."

"Some of us just wanted to stay by the fire and sing." Pam meekly replies.

"There's nothing wrong with gigging frogs or singing by the fire. Do either of you have any idea what the absolute top goal of pre-camp staff training is?" She angrily looks into our faces for an answer. I decide it's wiser to say nothing. "Obviously, neither of you do. It's to build cohesive staff unity, build friendships, and eliminate all competition making a safe place for individuals to grow, both campers and staff. In less than five minutes you two have effectively split my staff in two. I don't know what kind of a war you're waging between you, but you will not use my camp for your battleground.

"There was time tonight to do both activities, and people always have a choice as to the activities they choose to do. You forced the staff to choose not an activity but to support one or the other of you. I desperately need both of you here this summer, but if you pull a stunt like this again, you're gone. By the end of this week, I need to see you two cooperating and appreciating each other, or you'll have return plane tickets in your hands. I will not have malicious competition in my camp which creates contention of any kind. Do you both understand?"

I'm completely blown away, and I think Pam is too. We both tell her we understand.

She turns to Pam, "Take one of your canoes and give Terry a ride back to her unit, then you return to yours. I want you both to think carefully about your actions and what I've said tonight. And I'd better see a difference in the morning. Terry, you're teaching a breakfast, then Pam's doing first aid, followed by anyone interested in rock climbing and repelling with Rusty and Terry. Now go. I have some serious damage control to take care of."

It's my usual gray dawn again, and I'm on a trail. I sat on a rock last night outside our cabin until long after Dixon and Tracy had gone to bed. I cried and tried to reason out what I should do then cried buckets more. Mrs. Scott was right; my anger is fueling contention. I just don't know what to do about it. I wish there was someone I could talk to about it. Tom would tell me to talk to the Lord, but I haven't talked to Him for years since he let our parents die. Sometimes I wish He was there. All I can do is try harder.

I have all the food and equipment in unit 2 for cooking breakfast in a paper bag. This is my second trip from the lodge with all the climbing and repelling equipment. I want to be ready as soon as Pam finishes with her First Aid. I round a corner in the trail to spot Whisty, an AUL, looking up the side of the crumbly cliff.

"You're up early this morning Whisty," I try to say cheerfully.

"Yaa, you know, up with the birds to enjoy nature. Thought I'd take a little hike." She sounds a little sarcastic and doesn't take her eyes off the dangerous cliffs.

I try to follow where her eyes are looking, "I hope you're not thinking of hiking up the side of this mountain. That's extremely rotten rock up there. Nothing solid to hold on to or get a footing on. We're going to be doing some climbing with safety equipment later. You're welcome to join us."

"I'm not going to do anything dangerous; I only want to stretch my legs a little before breakfast." She turns and walks back around the bend I just came from.

I have just explained how to cook their breakfast when the air is shattered with a shrill, piercing scream. Before I can even move, Taylor runs into our cooking area yelling, "Whisty just fell down the mountain, and landed headfirst on a ledge."

A voice in my head starts telling me what to do. I loop the climbing ropes over my shoulder and grab my climbing harness as an afterthought. I charge toward Taylor motioning her to lead the way. Then I yell, "Pam, bring your First Aid Kit." I can sense all the staff is behind me. Taylor leads us right to the spot where I talked with Whisty earlier.

Taylor points up the mountain, "I saw her up there by those black shiny rocks. Her feet started sliding down the mountainside. She was trying to grab everything to hold on to. When she got to that area bulging out a little, her body came away from the mountain and she fell through the air landing on that ledge with her arm out in front of her. I think she might have hit her head. She was screaming until she hit. Then there was nothing."

The ledge is about twenty feet above us with nothing solid to climb on to get to it. The rocks to the side are all shiny crumbly black granite. I move along the trail about thirty feet to where the rocks are larger, and plants and some trees are growing going up the mountain. I study the area above the ledge and smile when I see a dead cottonwood clinging to the mountainside about twenty feet above Whisty. The base diameter is three feet, and it has a crotch about twelve feet up formed by two dead limbs reaching five feet high.

"Rusty, belay me!" I yell.

While I'll stepping into my harness, she stands close beside me, "Terry, there's nothing up there to get a piton into. You must have a fulcrum for me to belay you."

I answer with urgency, "I'm going to climb up the side with the rocks and foliage to about twenty feet above that cottonwood with the rope hooked on me. At that point, I'll traverse the slope." I'm pointing to where I'm going. "When I get to shinney rock, I'm going to try flipping the rope into the crotch. Then we have a fulcrum. That's the only way we'll be able to get Whisty off the ledge. When I throw the rope, I may slip. Take up my slack as fast as you can." As I start the climb, I bow my head and offer a quick silent prayer, Father if you're there, please help us save Whisty.

There are plenty of footholds and things to grab on the way up the side of the slide area. When I reach the spot to start the traverse, the difficulty climbs to eight. I slowly work my way forward while at the same time undulating the rope to keep it from snagging. Rusty is doing the same from the bottom. About ten feet from where I will try to loop the rope over the trunk into the crotch, I start bringing up slack, so I'll have something to swing. The rock is getting crumbly, making sure-footing difficult. I stop to get ready to turn our giant jump rope. Rusty signals her readiness on the ground. We lift and throw on a count of three. The loop in the rope sails up into the air.

I'm holding my breath; it's going to be close. On its downward arch, it just slides past the top of the dead limb heading down toward the crotch. I'm about to breathe when it catches on a small protruding dead limb about two feet down. It's got to settle into the bottom of the crotch. I undulate the rope in a panic at the same time yelling, "Tension!" All the slack must be taken out of the rope now.

Suddenly the ground beneath my feet gives way, and I'm sliding down the mountainside. There's a slight hesitation as the rope shears off the dead limb then the ground disappears from under my feet. I yell, "Fall!"

They've done fast work on the ground because I only free-fall five feet before I'm jerked to a sudden halt. I'm a pendulum swinging in the air below the old cottonwood tree. My biggest problem is I'm swinging upside down…I hate it when that happens.

I catch my breath enough to gather all my strength to bunch into a ball. Using the swivel on my harness, I twist to what I hope is right-side up. I shoot out my hands and feet and am so relieved I don't have to be lowered to the ledge headfirst. My belay team is now slowly lowering me to where Whisty is still not moving. I yell, "Pam she's not moving and a cut that goes from the top of her head to her ear above her eye is still bleeding."

I'm relieved the ledge is wide enough for me to move around. I hear Pam, "Terry, catch." I look over the edge to catch a missile Pam's thrown. "Take the wrapper off and put the whole dressing on the cut. Don't unwrap it, use it just like it is. Put pressure on the cut until the bleeding stops. You'll need to push against the other side of her head with your other hand. Don't let her head move. Her neck has got to be broken. While you're holding that in place, check for the rise and fall of her chest to make sure she's breathing." Pam makes this all look so easy when she demonstrates, but I feel like a five-year-old learning to ride a bike.

"Terry, what else do you see?"

"She's breathing awfully fast. Her left forearm has an extra joint. It's bent almost in half at a gruesome angle. All her bare skin is scratched badly, she didn't have much on. She must have slid face-first down the rocks before she was pitched into the air…I think the bleeding is stopped."

"Keep holding the dressing in place with one hand and make a cravat out of your 104. Tie it around her head to hold the dressing in place with the knot on the cut…I need to be up there.

"I know you do…Rusty, put a harness and a helmet on Pam. While you're making her climbing ready, I'll send the rope down and you can send up her First Aid Kit.

With a horror-stricken expression, Pam gasps, "Terry I could never get up there the way you did."

"You don't have to Pam. I did what I did, so you can do what you do. They are going to hoist you up here with the rope. All you need to do is hold the rope with both hands, lean back, put your feet on the wall, and walk up as they lift you."

Pam does a much more methodical head-to-toe exam than I did. She turns to look down at the waiting staff. "Does anyone in this unit have a bath towel we can use?" One of the ULs says yes and rushed off to her cabin. "I need two sticks an inch and a half in diameter and a foot long. Can you also put together a sweatshirt stretcher like we made yesterday?

Make the poles eight feet long and about two inches in diameter." After a quick discussion, the staff scatter in every direction to get the needed items. The first items to come up are two green willows for the arm splint.

Pam looks a little dismayed, "I was hoping they would be a little flatter."

I reach out my hand, "How thick do you want them?" I pull out my survival knife and quickly have them about three-fourths of an inch thick. Pam gives me a thankful smile. I'm thinking about the stretcher we made yesterday and ask the staff below for four sticks an inch thick and three feet long.

We've cut a width off the towel so it's the right thickness for Pam to make a neck collar. She directs me on how to hold Whisty's head in traction while she wraps the towel around her neck and securely tapes it. We take the stretcher and place one pole as tight against her body as we can get it. I put her head in traction again and Pam pulls on her hips while turning her more on her side. With our feet, we move the pole closer to her back. Very slowly while keeping the body in traction, we roll Whisty over one pole and onto the sweatshirts. It's a good thing she's not as tall as Pam and me. With the stretcher spread out, I lash two poles to the top and two to the bottom. I don't want the sides to collapse inward when we attach the rope. Pam is pleased with the extra support. We cut more strips out of the remaining towel and Pam runs strips across the top of Whisty to keep her from rolling from side to side. She is most concerned about any head movement, so one strip goes across Whisty's forehead.

I attach ropes to the stretcher, and we're ready to lower her to the ground. We can hear the wail of the ambulance as it makes its way up the mountain to camp while Whisty is being lowered. When Pam is down, she puts a log underneath the head of the stretcher to elevate Whisty's head. The ambulance crew comes bouncing their wheeled gurney over the trail to get to us. I've never seen Pam look so concerned.

"We got here as fast as we could," the EMT leading the gurney says. He looks over the situation, "Let's get that contraption off and get her on to our gurney, we'll get her down to the hospital PDQ."

Pam looks at him with fire in her eyes, "This woman has fallen forty feet down that mountain." The EMTs look at where she's pointing. "She has a concession, a fractured neck, probably a fractured back, a fractured arm, and a large laceration on her head. Her heart rate and respirations are highly elevated indicating a significant loss of blood. Before we begin any movement, she needs fluid. Will you please start an IV!"

The two ambulance attendants look at each other. Finally, the one who seems to be the leader says, "Miss., Mike, and I are only EMT Basic. We don't do IVs. Our paramedic got in a wreck on his way to come with us. They told us to pick up the girl and get her to the hospital as quickly as we can."

"Get your IV kit from your ambulance, and I'll start the IV," Pam says with urgency. They just stare at her. Showing more and more frustration Pam says, "I'm a paramedic. I work in an ER Trauma Center in a large hospital. Now go get that IV kit." The second EMT runs for the ambulance.

Once the IV has been started, Pam focuses on the EMTs again. This contraption is staying right where it is. As unorthodox as it looks, she is being splinted tighter than you'll ever get her on that gurney. You're not going to bounce her fractures over this trail. Take your stretcher back to the ambulance and position it for the lift. Put your backboard on it and be ready for us."

She then turns to our staff, "Terry and Rusty, I want you at the head on each side. I need four more carriers who are close to the height of Terry and Rusty, one in the middle and on the end of each side." While holding the IV bag in the air, she instructs us how to lift and then carry the makeshift stretcher so Whisty floats through the air. Once we're at the ambulance, Pam moves backward up inside the ambulance as we place our co-worker on the backboard attached to the gurney. Once strapped on, the EMT uses the hydraulic system to lift everything into the back of the ambulance.

The lead EMT looks at Pam, "Miss, would you please ride with us to the hospital? We think your friend would do better with you back here than either of us."

Pam looks at Mrs. Scott who nods her head in agreement, "I'll be right behind you in my car."

Pam starts moving equipment, "I'll get the ECG and BP monitors on. Where's the oximeter, and do you have some morphine I can drip into this saline? Open the radio for me so I can talk to the ER doc." The lead EMT answers her questions and closes the back doors. He hasn't even shut his passenger door when the ambulance is moving with lights and a siren.

I stand motionless seeing nothing but hearing the siren fade as they rush down the canyon. Long after the sound vanishes, I feel an arm around my shoulders. I turn to look into Rusty's searching eyes, "I think you did everything humanly possible to save her Terry, the rest is in someone else's hands."

It finally registers whom I'm talking with. I throw my arms around Rusty, "Thank you for being on the other end of my rope. If it weren't for you, I'd be in that ambulance or funeral wagon going down the canyon about now."

Laughingly she says, "You're welcome, Terry. You're the gutsiest person I know. I think that's what makes you such a brilliant climber—It was good for more than one thing. Mrs. Scott should be able to see that you and Pam can work together."

I pull back shocked, "How do you know about that?"

Her expression changes to one of concern, "Terry, it's no secret. Everyone in camp knows you and Pam are having issues."

"How?" I demand.

"You know the van that picked you up at the airport full of staff members, we were all on the same flight with you and Pam. The stop in your town was so short we were not allowed to debark. We all watched as you and Pam got on and brought the artic ice with you. Neither of you said a word the entire time you were on the plane. Last night made it obvious when both of you turned a simple conversation into a heated argument for no reason. I'm glad you can work together. We need you both at camp this summer."

I am so embarrassed. Tom is right. If I can't control my growing anger, I'm going to ruin my life. I hang my head in silence.

Rusty changes the subject, "Alright everyone, thanks for a great team effort. We'll all be praying for Whisty in the next few hours… I think it's time for lunch. The cooks are going to be so confused that we're not beating down the doors for food. We'll have free time this afternoon until dinner. I think we all need a break." She puts her arm back around me, "Come on Terry, let's go eat."

I finally look at her with tears in my eyes, "I'm sorry Rusty. After this morning my stomach won't let me eat right now. I just need some quiet." She nods her head in understanding and joins the rest of the staff heading toward the lodge.

I'm sitting on a log fifteen minutes up the trail behind my Adventurer cabin. I've got to figure this out. For the first time in over a year, my anger was gone when I was trying to help Whisty. Thinking of Whisty crumpled on the ledge brings back all the pain of my parent's death. Now the intense crushing anger is back, and I don't know what to do with it. I did utter a short prayer before I started my climb. My prayer was answered, at least she was still alive when they left for the hospital. I am so confused; why was the prayer not answered for my parents? And why when I think of the unfairness do my anger and agitation sore?

Maybe what happened today is the key. If I get involved in helping and put my whole mind there, I won't feel the anger. I also need to treat Pam like any other staff member. We don't seem to have an issue if we're not competing. No one can suspect I'm being torn apart inside. Only four more days until the campers arrive, then I'll be more than busy.

We are almost finished with dinner when Mrs. Scott and Pam return from the hospital. Rusty stands and says, "Give us an update and then we'll let you eat in peace."

Mrs. Scott turns to Pam, "You know more than I do Pam; you explain.

"When we arrived at the hospital an x-ray machine and the orthopedic doctor were waiting in the ER. Everyone wanted to cut her loose from our crude splinting, but I convinced them to wait until we had the x-rays. When the doctor looked at the films, I thought he was going to faint. Three of the vertebrae in her neck were crushed beyond repair. She had five more cracked vertebrae in her spine. The doc said they couldn't treat her at their hospital, so a life-flight chopper was summoned. They did have her blood type in their blood bank, so she received three pints while we waited. She didn't appear to have any internal injuries

"The most miraculous thing is she has feeling in all her limbs, and she can wiggle her fingers and toes. She has many surgeries and a rough time ahead, but if all goes well, she will live and will not be paralyzed from the neck down. We put her in the life-flight chopper with all our splinting still in place. After seeing the x-rays no one wanted to touch anything. Thank you for a life-saving team effort."

    Pam slips onto the bench across the table from me to sit with her unit, and Mrs. Scott sits next to her on the end. Once Pam has her plate piled high with food, she makes eye contact with me instead of eating, "Terry, Whisty regained consciousness just before the life flight arrived. She wanted me to tell you she's sorry she didn't listen when you told her not to climb the mountain. She wanted to prove she could do more than anyone else. She didn't need any of the fancy climbing gear. I told her you risked your life to save her using all that fancy gear. She said to tell you 'Thank you'. I want to thank you for doing what you did, so I could do what I did. Without you stopping the bleeding, she would have died. Without the splinting, she would be paralyzed." She breaks our eye contact and begins to eat.

CHAPTER 6

Around the edge of the parking lot are signposts for each unit, and a UL is standing next to it to welcome their campers for the summer. AULs and JLs have the responsibility of greeting girls as they step off their buses and helping them find their luggage and their unit. After the last straggling camper has found her new summer home, I head toward my out-back unit as a staff member and not a camper. I just know this will be a summer I will never forget.

As soon as Tracy, Sandy (the other junior leader), and I join the Adventurers, we began the trek to our unit area. We are the furthest camp from the lodge. It's nestled in a grove of majestic firs on the other end of the lake about a half-mile away. Each girl has a backpack and one or two suitcases or duffels, but no one complains as we walk. It's an honor to be in this unit; we have a reputation to uphold. The girls will take their gear to their cabins and be back at the lodge for dinner in less than an hour. I know this group has only three weeks to get in shape for the big two-week backpacking trip. Now is as good a time as any to start conditioning. I start a conversation with the last girl in line as I bring up the rear.

The next three days are fuller than I ever imagined. In addition to the regular camp activities of swimming, canoeing, eating in the lodge, and campfires, the "Adventurers" add more activities of their own: planning the backpacking trip, hiking at least five miles a day, and cooking at least one meal on an open fire. By the time the evening campfire is over, campers and staff alike fall into bed.

At the end of the third day after the campers are tucked in for the night, Dixie calls her "Adventurer" staff together. "There's a staff get-together tonight in the lodge if you want to go. We must always have one staff member here with the girls, but I'll do that tonight. I'm still working on the menus for our trip. They are due first thing in the morning. With our new transportation, it'll only take you ten minutes to get to the lodge instead of thirty if you paddle instead of hike. Go and have a good time."

I don't want to have another encounter with Pam tonight. I make a quick decision, "Dixie, I want to learn how to prep and order food, can I help you?" She looks at me with a question but nods her head to say yes. I plan to stay as far away from Pam as I can but tell no one what I'm doing. I look at Tracy and Sandy, "You two have a good time."

As tired as I am, my sleep is not restful. I wake and dress as the first gray light of morning is creeping into the sky. Maybe an early morning hike and a conversation with nature will bring some peace back into my life. The air is chilled by a light breeze when I head up the path that disappears into the thick woods behind their unit.

I love being up early, especially if I can be a part of the birds' wake-up call. I make my way along the dark trail for about fifteen minutes and am about to break into the clearing where I want to watch the sunrise when the air begins to swell with noise. There is just enough light to see now; it's the morning alarm for every bird in the entire woods to sing with all its might.

As if by a conductor's downbeat, the dead quiet of the night changes to a full orchestration of sound heralding the coming of day. I know the overture will last only about ten minutes but being enveloped in this wake-up call is one of my rarest treasures of life. I don't know how to measure the amount of sound which fills the air, but I'm sure if someone were with me, we would need to shout to hear each other. The thunderous chorus builds its own contagious excitement, and it swallows me.

As the symphony begins to die down, I sit on a fallen log and hold on to the feeling lingering inside. When the excitement fades away with the rising sun, the thoughts of why I have taken this walk began to organize themselves in my mind. What am I going to do about Pam and the angry, empty, lonely feeling I am still growing inside?

I pick up a stick and began to scratch in the dirt from my perch on the log. I try to formulate a workable plan. I desperately need this summer to be fun and meaningful. I let myself wonder for a brief instant if Pam is the cause of all my agitation and anger. That must be where it is coming from.

I don't want to compete with Pam. I also don't want to spend time with her. I especially don't want anyone to know how I feel.

I weigh everything in my mind and decide I will just try harder to treat Pam as I do everyone else. If we need to talk, I will just carry on a discussion as if she is any other staff member. Where possible, however, I will avoid being in the same place at the same time. I will get so involved and busy in my unit spending most of my time getting ready for the pack trip that the agitation and emptiness which seem to be growing should melt away.

Watching the sun lift its head above the horizon into the world, I know my "Me" time is close to an end. Walking back to my unit to shake sleeping campers out of their bags, I feel good about my plan for dealing with the summer.

Mrs. Scott burst my bubble at the end of breakfast in the dining hall. She announces, "All units need to be in the dining hall for the next five evening meals. You also need to plan on spending an extra half hour after the meal for singing practice. Normally it takes a couple of summers to cement new songs, but if we can spend learning time upfront for a few days, I think we can enjoy them this whole summer. It will also give our new campers a chance to learn the old favorites. I love the sound ringing off the logs of this rustic lodge when we have developed rich harmonies. We haven't done this for nine years. It is my deepest desire to hear it again." It dawns on me that my mother must have made the beautiful music in this room and around the campfire outside. It also comes crashing down on me that Pam and I will be working together every day.

I approach Mrs. Scott during meal clean-up, "Am I playing the piano and Pam leading the music during these practice sessions?" My heart sinks when she tells me yes. I don't want to appear to be dreading this situation, so I add, "The piano will need to be positioned so Pam can direct the whole dining room, and I can see her at the same time. Can we move the piano now?" Mrs. Scott's expression changes from one of disapproval to one of pleasant surprise. She helps me move the piano, then I join my unit.

After three post-dinner practices, I am amazed at the sound coming from our campers. I am also impressed with Pam's abilities to lead and sing harmony. She seems astonished I can easily play three and four-part harmonies without written music to every song. Some of my anger melts away as we work on the music. I try hard to concentrate on helping the girls learn to hear the rich harmonies and not on helping Pam. Once we get on our two-week backpacking trip, I should be free of her.

Leaving breakfast, the next morning, Dixie grabs hold of my arm, "Tracy and Sandy will you take our girls back to our cabins and start them on lashing? Terry, you're coming with me." We head across the dining hall toward Rusty and Pam. I hope this isn't another scheme to get the two of us working together. When Pam spots us, she looks as skeptical as I feel.

"This is a moment I've waited for since I joined the staff five years ago," says Rusty with a mischievous grin. Now I'm more than confused.

Dixie has the same grin, "The out-back units have the ropes course this afternoon, and you two are going to set up the obstacle course. Every time a unit goes there the course must be set up for the age and ability level of the girls. In the past five years, neither of you has ever been challenged in your age group."

Rusty takes over, "The challenges must be set up so one of you could make it through on your own with great difficulty. Then both of you must work together to get you both through. When the campers come, they will be in groups of four to help each other make it through." I remember this challenge well. I could always make it through by myself, but getting everyone else in my group to the finish line was a questionable task

"You two better get started, we'll all be there at 1:00 pm," Rusty says. Pam and I look at each other and then start running for the ropes course.

We stop to catch our breath when we arrive at the first obstacle. "Terry, the first part will be easy. We set each challenge to your max. I could never make the whole challenge without help here or there."

"Are you sure Pam? You always took first in the individual round."

"That's because I was better than anyone else in my group. I watched you on the mountain getting to Whisty; I've never developed the strength you have. Our real challenge will be getting both of us through your course."

At the rope swing to get across the stream, I raise the rope so it's a foot above my head. I can run, jump, and grab the knot at the bottom then sail across the water. As I'm securing the rope Pam is shaking her head. "What?" I ask.

"Most of the campers will never reach the rope let alone hold on to cross the stream. Most of us jump up to get our feet on the rope while we're gripping for dear life to hang on. I can do it by myself if I get a running start." I realize Pam is right. This course is not about me being amazing; it's about everyone working together so everyone succeeds.

"If I lower the rope part way, can you run and grab high enough you can sit on the knot? Then I will give you a giant push."

Pam considers for a few moments, "Maybe, let's try." After a few tries, we find the perfect height and move on to the stepping stones in the stream.

We move them so they are placed at my running stride. Pam's legs are almost as strong as mine from tennis, and she has no problem racing step for step down the six stones to cross the stream. Again, I can see that not everyone will be able to do this without help. "Pam, I think on this one I should go first and lay down one of the boards from the climbing wall to help you on your jump from the last stone to shore."

"Smart thinking Terry, then they'll know how to help those that can't make the jump. Now, how are you going to get me over that climbing wall? I know you can half run up it to reach the top. I'm just not quite there." I know Pam's right; most of the girls won't make it. I intently study the wall.

"Pam, kneel on one knee." She does as I ask, and I decide to take off the two top boards. It is still higher than my record jump, but with a knee boost or a hand boost, all the girls should be able to make it. Pam steps into my laced fingers and as she pushes off the ground, I lift her into the air. She easily makes it over the wall. Instead of dropping to the ground on the other side, she turns and reaches a hand down toward me. I jump, grab her wrist, and she helps me over the wall. All the out-back campers should be able to make it.

Neither of us has trouble on the log balance beam as we both run across. When we do it for real, Pam will walk beside me to help if necessary. Pam turns to me with questioning eyes, "Did you actually walk across the beam on your hands last year?"

I am a little embarrassed, "Yeah, I did. I'm afraid I was being a bit of a show-off. It was not much of a challenge course for me."

"I can understand that. I think you should do it again in our duo. You walk on your hands, and I'll do cartwheels. I'll be your safety net and you be mine. If I start to fall, push me away from the beam so I don't fall on it."

It hits me like lightning; I'm working with Pam and all my agitation and hate are gone. It's what happened when we worked together to take care of Whisty. I'm not going to dwell on it; I'll simply put my head back into this challenge course.

Pam is facing the climbing tree, "Terry, I can do this but I'm really slow getting myself up into the tree. If you could give me a boost, it would go much faster."

"I'll give you the boost, wait until you are about ten feet up, and then I'll start. When I get to you, I'll move around to the opposite side of the tree to pass you, ring the bell, and start down. You should be right behind me ringing the bell." We practice her boost into the tree and her landing back on the ground.

Next, we face the monkey bars. Pam starts on them reaching for one rug at a time with one hand and bringing the other up to hold with it. I can see she is moving dead weight with every new reach. "Pam, why don't you swing, It's much easier."

She answers through gritted teeth, "I don't know how. My dad would never let me play on them, He was afraid I would get hurt and not be able to play tennis." She drops to the ground. "Show me how."

I climb to the starting stand and reach out with one hand three rungs down. I let my feet swing down while I reach with my free hand four rungs down. When I grab that rung, I let go of my trailing hand and swing forward again. It takes about five swings and I'm across the bars.

"Terry, you make that look so easy. I'm sure I don't have enough strength to do that."

"It's not so much strength as it is momentum. Climb back up there and I'll help you." Once she's in the position I take hold of her waist, "Count to three, let go with your trailing hand, and let your feet swing forward. Keep reaching forward with your free hand until you grab a rung. Count." She counts and lets her body swing forward until she grabs three rungs down. "Let go of your trailing hand and swing again." This time the swing is freer, and she reaches four rungs and almost immediately lets go of her trailing hand to swing forward again. She finishes leaving my help behind. She ends up standing on the support ladder with the largest grin I have ever seen. Without a word, she swings like a pro back across the bars and climbs to the ground.

"What's next?'

The mention of tennis and her father shoot ice through me like a jagged dagger. All the anger and agitation return in full force. I fight with everything I possess to retain control and keep my voice with no emotion

"The 'Spider Web' and I think we can both do it at the same time." We both begin climbing up the net with foot squares. It gradually slopes up to a large rope eight feet above the ground and then slopes down the other side. Each side is twelve feet square. We begin three feet apart and three feet off the ground.

I have always thought the last four challenges were way below the difficulty of the first obstacles in the course. We easily crawl with hands and feet over the spider web, roll under and vault over the ten parallel logs suspended four feet off the ground, walk fast almost to the point of running the twenty-five yards on two-foot stilts, and finally strap our legs together for the three-legged run back to the starting of the course.

As I am bending over releasing the Velcro strap holding our legs together, Pam whispers, "I am sorry about my father."

I quickly look up at her. I've rehearsed this scenario so many times the words come before I can even think about them, "Pam, we've been in competing situations our whole lives, and I've always felt we played fair with each other. You and your father cheated to win at the State Tennis Finals."

"Terry, I felt bad about what happened."

"I could tell you felt exceptionally remorseful while you were laughing and accepting all the congratulations and hugs after the last point. I'll bet your father even carried home the first-place trophy you stole from me. I was not prepared to defend myself against the two of you."

"What you did in our American Problems debate wasn't exactly the epidemy of honor. You buried me ten feet under."

"I was just following the new rules for engagement you put in place at the match."

"I'll bet you left class, high-fiving all your friends walking down the hall celebrating how you buried me alive," Pam says.

"No, after the debate was the most upsetting part of my day. I knew I had put you down in front of the class, but I received no satisfaction from it. I lost so much more than I gained. I shattered my code of moral ethics. I never treat people that way, and I will never do it again no matter how they treat me."

I hear both out-back units racing through the woods. "Pam let's cloque our contempt for each other so we don't get fired, and let's smash the record for the duo obstacle time so no one will ever be able to break it."

Pam looks bewildered but has no time for a reply as we're swarmed by campers.

Within minutes, forty girls and their leaders are gathered around the rope swing. I even spot Mrs. Scott in the back of the group. We've got to make this look good. I whisper to Pam, "After you swing across the water, you go first down the stepping-stones and put the board in place for me to walk on for the last step." Pam nods in agreement.

Rusty steps out from the group, "Have you had time to set this course?"

Pam answers with no hesitation, "The course is set for Terry's max with a few minor adjustments so the rest of us have a chance to finish the course with a little help from each other."

Rusty speaks to the whole group, "Terry will do the individual challenge first, then Pam and Terry will do it together. Watch closely to pick up any tips you can. Terry, let me know when you're ready."

"I'll get a drink of water, and I'm ready." I don't need a drink, but I do need a few minutes to calm myself down. If I'm too hyped, I could make some stupid mistake and blow the whole thing."

I take the rope and walk as far away from the stream as I can. On Rusty's signal, I take three running steps and jump as high up on the rope as I can grab with both hands. I easily swing over the stream and let go as I reach the top of the arc. As soon as my feet touch the ground, I'm running for the stepping-stones. My momentum carries me through every obstacle without losing any speed. When I approached the beam, I debate walking on my hands but ran across instead saving the stunts for our duo.

When I cross the finish line everyone is cheering. Rusty finally quiets the excited campers, "Terry, you beat your record last year by four minutes, and the difficulty is twice what it was then. I'm impressed." There's another round of applause and noise. "We'll give you fifteen minutes to catch your breath, and we'll start the duo."

"I just need another drink and I'm ready. Might as well use the adrenalin while I still have it." I turn to look at Pam to see if she's ready. She's staring in stunned silence. "Pam, let's do it while I'm warmed up."

She moves to the rope and starts to reach, I move behind her and put my hands on her waist while whispering, "I'm going to boost you before you grab, it'll be easier to bring your legs up to sit on the knot. On the other side, all you need to do is pull up with your arms, spread your legs, and let go. Then run for the stepping-stones." I pull her back for the push and instantly decide I'll grab higher, and we'll go together. I let Pam jump down first while I make a swing back over the water and then to shore. I'm fast on her heels. She barely gets the board in place for me to walk on.

I move with my back to the wall, lace my fingers together to make a foothold, and dip into a slight squat to use my legs. When I lift Pam, her hands shoot above the wall, and she catches it on the way back down. She quickly turns and extends an arm toward me. I jump to catch her wrist. All she needs to do is hold while I walk up the wall until my other hand is on the top board. She lets go, and I'm over.

We move quickly to the balance beam and the crowd is doing the same. I move to a spotting position on the side, and she begins her cartwheels. The girls are crazy with excitement. At the end of her pass, we trade places, and I walk across on my hands with my feet making strange movements in the air.

Before we even stop at the climbing tree, I lift Pam to the first branch and she's on her way up. As soon as she's out of my way, I begin. I pass her on the opposite side of the tree, ring the bell, and pass her on the way back down. She's picking up speed, She's on the ground only a minute after I am. We start at opposite ends of the monkey bars and pass in the center. We finish the Spider Web by doing a summersault at the edge to land on our feet. We sail through the remainder of the challenges sprinting the three-legged run.

Again, Rusty has trouble quieting the noisy group. "Wow, I've never seen a team function together like that. You've beaten the old team record by ten minutes. I doubt if anyone will ever top that. You even took the time to show off…

"Our afternoon's moving on, and we have much to do to be on time for dinner. Pam, you come with me and the Explorers, and we'll do the rest of the ropes course. Terry, you stay here and encourage your Adventurers. Then our units will trade places. See you all at dinner."

My eyes follow Pam as she leaves with her unit. My emotions are so mixed up. One minute she's so easy to work with, and the next I can't stand to be anywhere around her. I'm still furious she cheated in our tennis match.

The next few weeks are packed with activities preparing us for the backpacking trip. What I don't understand is why we are doing so many joint evening activities with the Explorers. If we're not eating dinner in the lodge, we're with them. This is my third year in an out-back unit, and in the first two years, we never saw the other unit until the last week of camp after our backpacking trips.

It's been three days since our obstacle course adventure, and we're heading to a sandy beach on a lake about two miles from camp. We've prepared foil-wrapped chickens and vegetables to cook in pits for our dinner. When we arrive, the Explorers are already there waiting for us.

Dixie turns to me, "We're all yours Terry. Teach us how to cook our dinner in the ground." I knew I would be teaching our unit but am surprised to be giving instructions to both units. During the cooking and eating, I never make eye contact with Pam. I wonder if she's as uncomfortable with being together as I am.

Once the girls bury the food in hot coals covered with sand, Dixie organizes another fire-building group. The Explorers are designated to find and bring logs to sit on and the Adventurers are relegated to finding enough firewood for the evening campfire. It's hard to tell if the girls are impressed with this new way of cooking, but they're all excited at how delicious it tastes. As the eating is ending, the campers begin asking for after-meal singing. Pam automatically stands to take charge.

I silently slip away and return to cover the pits we cooked in. It's one thing to leave a fire circle with sitting logs, but unacceptable to leave open cooking pits for others to step in. I've only begun when I feel a hand on my shoulder, "Mind if I help you?" Dixie asks as she picks up the other shovel. "You're smart to get this done before it's completely dark. I'm sure we'd be the first to fall in them when we hike back to our beds."

We're not far from the fire but out-of-sight and out-of-mind. Pam is trying to get the girls to sing the three-part song, "Dona". It's a cleverly written Latin song of peace with three different melodies woven together. Pam's frustration is surfacing, "Isn't there one of you that knows the second or third parts well enough to not be thrown off by the other melodies? I heard the other out-back unit singing this song all the time last summer.

Alison comes to the defense of the Adventurers, "Our part leaders are off doing clean-up. When Terry and Dixie sing parts, it's easy to sing this song."

Pam's stunned, "Terry sings?"

Alison proudly answers, "She can sing any part and can harmonize to any melody. She makes any group she's in sound good." She then yells, "Terry and Dixie, we need you at the fire circle." I smile inside.

Dixie yells back, "We're on our way." When we enter the firelight, Dixie reorganizes the group. "If you want to sing the second melody, sit in this area with me, and if you want to learn the third sit in that area with Terry." The whole group quickly rearranges. Dixie suggests we sing all the parts together and then begin it as if we are singing a round. Pam can tell she's needed more to be the singing leader of the first group rather than a conductor and joins her group on their log. When we finally sing the song in parts, it's as beautiful as I have ever heard it. At this moment,

I'm glad both units are together in song. It makes a richer sound. I love beautifully harmonized music; it wraps itself around my heart.

Sharing my love of the outdoors with the girls is an exciting part for me. I teach them the names of flowers and plants, always pointing out which ones are edible. It had been a family tradition that we went on a survival vacation every summer. My brothers made sure we continued the tradition after mom and dad died. I am now discovering teaching survival is as much fun as doing it myself.

Early on in our hikes, I get my campers playing a postcard game. Each person looks for a nature scene that could be on a postcard and points it out to the rest of the group. All the girls in the unit vote to decide if they think it's postcard material. If a majority agrees, a picture is taken and displayed on the cabin walls. Their postcards cover scenes ranging from panoramic mountain-top views to a lupine wildflower that has captured a dew droplet in its leaf cluster and displays it as a sparkling royal diamond in the early morning sun.

The more time we spend together, the more I like being with "my" campers. When nighttime comes around, I focus on enjoying the singing whether we're in the lodge or around a fire with the Explorers. Three weeks pass fast, and finally, the prep time is over.

I sit by the fading campfire after everyone else has gone to bed and try to envision tomorrow. The buses will be in the parking lot early, and before the sun lights the sky, we will be off to the Red Rock Wilderness for our two-week backpacking trip. The girls in my unit are excited and ready. I'm ready. I wonder if I will even be able to sleep as I pour water over the last remaining coals, but I know that I had better try.

"Terry, Wake up! Our campers are going to beat you to the bus. We may have to leave you here," Dixie yells.

I wake with a start when I hear Dixie call my name. I fly to the door of our staff cabin as Dixie walks out. I relax a little when I realize she is on her way to wake the girls and is giving me a tough time. I turn back to look at the beds and see that I am the last staff member to roll out. Tracy's and Sandy's sleeping bags are empty. They must be in the shower. I had better get there before the campers, or I will be the last one on the bus.

Getting ready this morning is easy; my backpack is packed. I only need to shower, slip into my clothes, which are laid out, stuff my sleeping bag, and strap it onto my pack. Because everyone is excited, it takes little time to have all the girls on the trail to the lodge and the bus. When I can see the parking lot, I see two buses. For the first time, it registers that the Explorer unit will be going out today also. For an instant, I wondered where they are going but don't give it much thought. When we get to the buses, Dixie stops the group to give instructions. "Put your packs under the bus in the luggage area, and then go to the lodge for breakfast. The cooks got up extra early to give you your last healthy meal. Eat heartily. For the next two weeks, you'll have to eat your own cooking."

"Dixie, which bus do we put our packs on?" comes the question from Alison, the first camper in line.

"Our unit will ride on the second bus, but it doesn't make any difference which one you put your pack on. They're both going to the same place."

I can't believe what I heard, "Dixie, did you say that the Explorers are going to the same place that we are?" My excitement nosedives. Pam can't be going where I'm going!

"Terry, didn't you know that? It's been the plan from the beginning. You look like you've been hit over the head with a baseball bat. Is there a problem?"

I am slow to answer; my heart feels like it's lying on the floor being stomped on. I try to casually comment, "No problem…I guess I assumed we would be going to different places since the Out-Back Units have never gone to the same place in the past."

I change the subject before too much of my disappointment comes through. I raise my voice and say, "Come on ladies. Let's get these packs on the bus before our breakfast gets cold." I led the way to the luggage doors of the second bus where I put my pack and help to stow all the others.

After all the packs are aboard, I slowly make my way toward the lodge. All desire for food has gone, and I'm fighting down my anger. But I know I had better eat anyway. I am a little startled when I feel Dixie's arm slip around my shoulders. "Terry, I hope you're not too disappointed, and I'm sorry you didn't know we're going with the other unit. It's going to be such a neat experience for the girls that neither Out-Back Unit wanted to go anywhere else. That's why we've been having all our evening activities together, so the girls could get to know each other. Mrs. Scott thought combining forces would be a good idea. She said it even gave her a good excuse to come on the trip. Look at the bright side Terry. We'll continue to have our singing sessions with our combined units. I think we'll be working closely with the other staff." That's all I need, to spend more time with Pam. It feels like I'm walking into a nightmare.

As we walk through the door into the dining hall, I don't know if I am going to cry or scream. Why? Why? My thoughts race in desperation. Why does Pam have to be in the middle of the things I love the most? How is this pack trip ever going to work?

"Terry, Terry, Terry!" It's not until the third time they shout my name that my mind registers someone is shouting at me. A table full of Adventures is motioning and calling to me. "Terry, come and eat with us."

I slip away from Dixie and make my way to the table, "I don't know. This table looks pretty rowdy." It's hard to put on a front of having fun when my insides want to scream, but there is no way I want to let anyone know what I'm feeling. As I try to force down food and joke with my campers at the same time, I realize this could be my salvation again. I will spend all the time I can with my kids, and simply avoid as much contact with Pam as possible. This resolution eases my inner turmoil a little, and I smile as the group at our table heads for our bus.

Right on schedule, the buses pull out of the parking area on their way to the Red Rock Wilderness. After an all-day ride, we'll be at the trailhead. One more night and we'll be putting our packs on and hiking down into the slot canyon. Once the buses are on their way, Alison yells from the front of the bus, "Dixie, tell us what it's going to be like, this little hike in the Wilderness. One of the kids in the Explorers said that we were going to the desert. Are there any mountains, or trees, or water?"

Dixie walks to the front of the bus to use the mic. "It sounds like you've heard just enough rumors that you're finally ready to listen. We are going to the desert, but it won't be like anything you ever pictured in the desert. You are also going to see more water than you've ever seen on a backpacking trip. We are going into the San Pitch Canyon. All the canyons in that area were carved by rivers, and they are called slot canyons because of how deep and steep they are. In some places the canyons are wide and spread out, in others, they're narrow enough to touch both sides at the same time. Most of the rock in the area is sandstone, and because it's porous, some of the canyons are cut extremely deep. There will be places where when you stand in the stream and look up, the walls will extend straight up for five hundred feet. It'll be different than standing on the top of a mountain, but it will be a feeling that you will never forget."

"Where's all of this water coming from if we're going to a desert canyon?" Someone calls out from about the middle of the bus.

"Remember, I told you all of these canyons were made by streams. The San Pitch still has its river, only at this time of year the water level is low. We are going to hike in the bottom of the canyon in and out of the river going downstream. There are only a few places you can get a car or bus anywhere near the river or canyon floor. We are starting in the upper part of the canyon and hiking downstream for about thirty miles. The only way out of the canyon is back the way we came or where the road breaks into the canyon at the place we'll finish our trip. The buses will be waiting for us at the trail's end."

Chris fires a question, "It must be hard hiking if it's going to take two weeks to hike thirty miles. How far do we go in a day?"

Dixie smiles and continues, "It's not that hard. We'll cover most of the downstream mileage in three days. When we camp at the end of the third day, we'll only be about five miles from the end. We'll be up a side canyon at Big Spring, where we'll base camp for the rest of the time. There are so many side canyons to explore from there we could spend a month. We'll be close enough to the end that we're not even going to carry all the cooking fuel. About mid-trip, we'll send a couple of leaders down the river to the camp car to trade empty cans for full ones. It's going to be a neat trip. You'll love every minute of it."

By an unknown pre-set signal, the quiet attention erupts into animated conversation. Everyone wants to talk about what she thinks the trip will be like. Dixie smiles at their excitement and seems to know her speech is over. She makes her way to the back of the bus, answering questions from every seat she passes.

When she finally reaches the rest of our unit staff, she flops into her seat and says, "This is going to be a good trip, I can feel it. I remember the first time I came to hike the narrows. I tried and tried to picture in my mind what it would be like. I didn't even come close."

The excitement and noise level on the bus stays high all through the morning until the bus stops for lunch. After lunch, there seems to be another preset signal for everyone to sleep. Within a half-hour, there is total silence on the bus. I fight sleep again, but my short nights get the best of me. I join my unit slumber.

I am still asleep when the bus rolls to a stop at our trailhead. Sandy put her hand on my shoulder and says, "Terry, wake up. We're here. You're not going to be able to sleep tonight."

I groggily reply, "I don't know what it is about buses, but they sure put me to sleep. As for tonight, right now I feel like I could go back to sleep this very minute and sleep for three days." I stagger down the aisle trying hard to completely wake up. When I step off the bus, the setting sun hits me in the eyes. When I can finally see, I can't believe the transformation. In those hours I had slept, the country has become a whole new world. Instead of green, there are now mountains of red rock. The last light of the sun brings out every shade of red I have ever seen. As I looked around trying to take it all in, I say to no one in particular, "Wow, is this ever going to be postcard country."

"Terry, come out of your daze. We've got to get these buses unloaded and camp set up before we lose all of our light." Dixie is shouting at me from the luggage compartment as she hands packs to campers.

In an instant, I'm by her side. "Sorry. Let me do this, and you show the kids where we're setting up camp. I think I'm awake now."

Dixie gives me a smile and the pack in her hands. Stepping away from the bus, she picks up a box marked "Adventurer's Food" and calls back to me. "I'll send some kids back for the other food boxes. Follow them with your stuff when all the packs are off and accounted for. It's a good thing we don't have to cook much of the dinner tonight. It's going to be dark before we even get camp set up."

I'm more than ready when Sandy and three campers return for the food boxes. "Where's our camp?" I ask.

"Not very far," says Sandy.

Alison takes over, "Terry, you're going to love it. It's behind those house-size rocks on green grass by the river. Sandy's even got your tent set up right by ours."

"Well, quit talking about it, and show me where it is." I throw on my pack, pick up the last food box, and follow my escorts through the rock maze.

When we round the last huge boulder, the ground opens into a grassy clearing that gently slopes down to a small stream. The rising tents are silhouettes against an almost black sky. I breathe a little sigh of relief when I can see there is only room for one unit in this area. There is a roaring campfire in the center of the tents, and people are busy putting a cook-less dinner together. We make our way to the fire and put down the boxes. I turn to Sandy and say, "Lead the way to our home."

The next morning before the sun peeks over the East Mountains, both units are at the stream's edge ready for an adventure into the unknown. Mrs. Scott sets her pack down by a low table-sized rock and then climbs on top of it. "It's been years since we've taken a group from Lightning Mountain Camp down these canyons. Dixie is the only other person in this group besides me that's hiked down this watery trail. I need to give you a few instructions before we get started."

There is a low moan from the group, and at least half of the fifty people take off their backpacks. "We won't be here long, but there are some things you must know about canyon hiking. Your unit will be hiking as a group. The Explorers will lead out this morning. For the most part, you need to hike in a single file, following the person in front of you. Each of you should have your walking stick and should use it. Once we are confined to walking in the water, we'll never know what we're stepping on or in. Your stick will help give you balance and help you find holes. If you'll walk behind the person in front of you, only your leader will be the one to disappear into a hole.

"The air will be hot, but the water will always be cool. Believe it or not, our biggest danger, even more than poison ivy, rattlesnakes, scorpions, and tarantulas, down in the canyons is hypothermia. We'll be keeping a watch out for it, but you need to be aware of what's happening to your own body. Please watch for these signs: uncontrollable shivering, stumbling, poor coordination, confusion or slurred speech, and fatigue or weakness. If you see any of these signs in yourself or anyone around you, please let your leaders know."

Alison starts staggering around bumping into people and making strange jabbering sounds. Everyone laughs when Dixie interrupts Mrs. Scott, "Alison, sit down. You're not even wet yet." Sitting down, Alison pretends surprise.

Mrs. Scott throws Alison a disgusted look and finishes her speech. "We want you to all have an enjoyable time. Just please stay aware of everything around you."

She turns and speaks directly to the Explorer UL, "Rusty, take your girls and get started."

A shout goes up from the group, and Mrs. Scott climbs down from the rock. I can't believe we're finally on our way. I have looked forward to this for so long, that it almost doesn't seem real.

Dixie begins organizing our unit, "Let's give them five minutes, then we'll start. Terry, you walk upfront with me. Tracy and Sandy, you bring up the rear. Let's not get too spread out. If there's a problem in the back, let us know so we can slow down or stop."

We watch the Explorers disappear around the bend, and Dixie finally gives the signal to load up. I am following close behind Dixie as we start down the trail which runs right next to the stream. Alison is in line right behind me, obviously not wanting to miss a thing. "Dixie, I thought you said we'd be walking in the river. This looks like dry ground to me."

"Be patient, Alison. You'll have your feet wet in five minutes. Before we're through you'll long for a dry path."

Dixie's words are not long in being fact. When we round the bend, the trail leads right into the stream as the canyon walls closed in and cut off the banks. Someone from the middle of the line calls out, "Terry, everywhere I look it's a postcard. We could play the game of who could find a picture that doesn't look like a postcard."

I laugh, "We better make sure we take lots of pictures. This is something you could never explain with words. If you could, I'm not sure anyone would believe you."

As the walls get closer and higher, the whole group becomes silent. I moved close to Dixie to talk without sharing my thoughts with the whole group. "Dix, it's fantastic in here with the red rock cliffs going up hundreds of feet on both sides of us. I'm excited, but I also feel funny. I feel a little trapped. If anything should happen, there's no way out."

"Terry, that's why the whole group is quiet. I think it's a little fear, fear of the closeness, fear of being so small when the canyon's so big, and fear of the unknown. I remember the feeling from the first time I was here, and I have a little of it now. Give us a half-hour, and it'll be gone."

"Dixie, I've done enough camping in the desert to know about flash floods. What happens if it rains while we're in the canyons?"

"Good question, Terry. We've been keeping a close eye on the weather, and it's supposed to stay good, but we also must keep an eye on the sky. If it even looks like rain, we find high ground and stay there until we're sure the water level's stable."

Ann, the girl behind Alison, sounds like she is beginning to shake the canyon fear response. "Terry, look at those flowers growing right out of the side of the wall."

I look up, "It looks like a hanging garden. The whole side of that huge flat rock has flowers growing out of every crack. Those bright red ones that look like they are hanging by an arm or tail are Monkeyflowers. Look at those little green ones that have the stems growing right out of the middle of the leaf. That's Miner's Lettuce. If we find some growing low enough, we can have a mid-morning snack."

Pointing near the base of the rock, I exclaim, "Look how beautiful. The small greenish-white flowers are desert orchids. There must be a spring where the water is seeping along in the ground and has found a way out through the cracks. I think that's worth three postcards."

I am thankful for my walking stick as we make our way through the water. The stream is muddy from all the hikers in front of us, and my stick gives me a sense of security in knowing what's there before I step. Sometimes the stream bed is flat with small gravel under my feet. At other times I make my way over or around large boulders. We have been hiking long enough that all fear from the group for the canyon seems to be gone, and we are about to catch the tail end of the Explorers ahead of us.

Alison is becoming so comfortable she begins walking out of the established trail to hike side by side with her friends and to explore the walls of the canyon closer. On a glance back over my shoulder, I see her over on the other side of the stream. "Alison, you're not following directions very well. You need to stay in line. On top of that, you don't even have a walking stick."

Alison pretends to not hear but makes her way back to the line. She then starts working her way forward to walk beside me. At this point, the canyon gets narrower, and we are now walking in water about two feet deep. "All this stuff about walking in a line is dumb," she says. "There's plenty of room. We'd have a much better time if we walked as a group. I can't hear anything anyone says when we're so spread out. I don't need a stick either, I'm not a pansy. I think I'll show Dixie how it's done." She starts taking large steps to make a swing out around Dixie when she slips and disappears into the water out of sight.

Dixie and I both watch her go down and have almost reached her before she goes completely under. I'm feeling the bottom with my stick, "It drops off right here." In my next step, I am up to my waist. Reaching down into the water, I grab hold of Alison's pack. Dixie has stepped into the hole on the other side and has hold of Alison's arm. We both pull quickly and hard to get Alison's head above the water. She comes up coughing and choking, blood then begins covering her forehead.

Dixie gives orders as Alison begins to move. "Get her over to the shallow, quick. Terry, take her pack off."

I unbuckle Alison's waist strap and take her pack off as we walk. It is only about ten feet to the side with a rock for her to sit down on. By the time we get there, Alison has stopped choking and is just breathing hard, but her face is covered with blood.

"Terry, you've got our unit's first aid kit, haven't you?" asks Dixie.

"I do, but it's in the middle of my pack. Hang on one minute, and I'll get it. Sandy, set Alison's pack down on that other rock."

I hand Alison's pack to Sandy and am about to slip off my own when Pam's voice behind me says, "Get ours. It's in the top zipper of my pack. It's always ready in case of an emergency, even during the middle of the day."

I turn to face Pam who is turning to make the back of her pack accessible. I unzipped the top compartment and pull out a first aid kit. I am about to open it and go to work when Pam takes it out of my hands and says, "I don't think it's as bad as it looks." She opens the kit, looks for a spot to set it down, and turns back to me. "Terry, hold this will you?" Not even waiting for an answer she puts the kit in my hands and takes out several three-inch gauze squares. She folds one in half and put it on Alison's head. "A little pressure right here ought to take care of this quickly. Alison, how do you feel?"

"Dumb!"

Both units have gathered now, and everyone laughs a little at her lengthy answer. While Pam looks straight into Alison's eyes and presses hard on her forehead, she asks again, "I don't mean how you felt about what you did. How does your body feel?"

"My head hurts a little. But mostly I'm cold, wet, and embarrassed."

Pam pulls the compress away from Alison's head and inspects the cut. "I think it's stopped bleeding. The cut's not too bad; it's only about half an inch long."

"Where did all that blood come from? I thought she was dead or at least dying right here in the middle of this stream." Dixie says.

Pam answers Dixie's question as she pulls the sides of the cut together with a butterfly bandage and puts a Band-Aid over the top of it. "Little cuts on the head always bleed lots. If they're wet, the blood mixes with the water, and it looks catastrophic."

"A little face wash with my trusty '104', and you'll be as good as new." Pam pulls her handkerchief from her back pocket, dampens it in the stream, and cleans up Alison's face.

"Alison, you look like a new person," Dixie says.

"Dixie, you don't need to say anymore. I can feel what's coming next. 'Let's have a little chat about this adventure.' I've learned enough lessons for me and everyone else here. I still feel dumb."

"It sounds like you got the point. I won't say any more except we're going to find you a walking stick."

Dixie turns to talk to the snickering group, "I hope it's enough lessons for all of you." She changes the subject, "There isn't a place to stop here. If you take your packs off, you'll have to set them in the water. Tracy and Sandy, you lead out and take the unit downstream to the next wide spot in the canyon. We'll stop there and eat an early lunch. We'll follow you as soon as we get Alison on her feet. We'll let her rest and get dry there, or she'll be our first example of hypothermia, too."

Pam is packing up her first aid kit when Dixie says, "I'm sure glad you're a trained paramedic. They tell me you're the Doc of the Explorers."

"I've worked at the hospital in the emergency room long enough that they let me do the emergency stuff all the time. It comes in handy, especially at times like this. Terry, will you put my kit back in my pack, so I can be ready for the next emergency?" Pam hands the kit to me and turns around.

Throughout the whole first aid session, I have not said a word, but feel increasingly like I've taken second place again. This is my unit, Alison is my camper, and Pam rubbed it in hard that I had not been prepared.

I think, so she can take care of emergencies, she doesn't have to make me look like I can't do a thing. I feel completely deflated when I hear Dixie say, "Thanks, Pam, it's a good thing you were in the back of your line, and you had your first aid kit handy. We couldn't have done it without you. You know your stuff."

CHAPTER 7

I watch Pam leave at the end of the Explorers, and then our Adventures slowly move ahead with all the girls chattering. Watching Pam leave, I whisper to myself, "Good riddance. She's going back to her unit where she belongs." In a few minutes, they are all out of sight as they round the steep-walled canyon bend.

I look around to see if there isn't someplace to sit for a few minutes when Alison stands up from her rock seat and announces, "I'm ready to go."

Dixie takes hold of her arm to steady her, "Are you sure? You've had a hard bump. Are you dizzy at all?"

"I don't feel great, but I'm okay."

"Walk around here a little. If you feel alright, then we'll put your pack on you," Dixie directs.

Alison walks around a little and then walks over to her pack. "Let's go. If I walk around much, I might find another hole."

Both Dixie and I smile then help her put on her pack. Dixie says, "Alison stay right behind me, and Terry will be right behind you. With the canyon so narrow through here, there are lots of deep holes."

Alison shakes her head, "Don't worry about me. I'm through being a trailblazer. I'll let you find all the drop-offs."

Alison pauses and speaks again, "Thanks for pulling me out of that hole. When I was under the water, I could feel the bottom with my hands and knees, but I couldn't get my feet under me to get up. That was a scary feeling."

We walk along in silence for a while when Alison pulls a question from nowhere. "Terry, why do all the staff call their handkerchiefs '104's'?"

Both Dixie and I chuckle as I answer, "That little piece of material is so versatile it's supposed to have at least one hundred and four uses. Every time someone uses it for something new, they mention it as if they are counting, but no one keeps track."

Looking at Alison's wet pack from the back, I comment, "I sure hope you put everything in plastic bags like you were told to do. If you didn't, the entire contents of your pack are drenched."

Alison doesn't even turn around or slow down as she answers, "That much I did listen to."

We go back to silent walking, and thoughts of Pam invade my mind again. Why does she have to keep being in the middle of my life? My anger level soars higher every time we interact. I sure wish I could figure out a way to just pretend she doesn't exist.

I don't get to ponder the idea too long because Dixie calls out, "I think I hear voices."

All three of us strain to listen, and then I say, "Dixie you've got good ears. I think I might hear them too."

"Sound doesn't carry very well in these winding canyons. They must be just around the turn." Dixie says.

As we round the bend, Alison taps Dixie on the pack with her new walking stick. "Miss Rabbit Ears, you were right. There they are all stretched out on the green grass. I can't believe the sides of this canyon just suddenly move back, and there's a grassy picnic area."

Dixie smiles, "I ordered it, especially for you, Ali."

We move to the dry bank to travel downstream about one hundred yards and then climb up the embankment to join the others on the grassy shelf. I take off my pack and look around. I am trying to decide if this is a postcard picture with the green grass, red rock, and lunching girls when I catch Pam in the corner of my eye.

Pam is on the other side of the meadow at the edge of the grass trying to make her way through rocks and high bushes. My full attention is drawn to Pam, and I have an uneasy feeling that something is wrong. I study Pam's movements as the uneasiness swells. When the realization hits me, I scream at the top of my voice, "Pam! Stop!"

Everyone, including Pam, stops dead still while I take quick giant running steps in Pam's direction. On my way, I yell again, "Don't move!"

I stop at the edge of the grass about five feet away from Pam. She has not moved a muscle including her outstretched hand. No one else had moved either. Fifty pairs of eyes are locked on me, and there is dead silence waiting for the worst. I shake my head and speak, "Look hard at those bushes you're about to push aside to walk through."

Pam's hand is extended, and in another step, she would have pushed the leafy bushes aside to make a path through. She looks intently at the branches she is about to push away, turns white, and gasps, "Oh my gosh!" jerking her hand back.

She looks at all the foliage around her and carefully begins to backtrack her footsteps.

Everyone is still bound in a trance except Mrs. Scott, who has made her way through the lunching campers to my side. "Terry, what's the problem?"

"See those bushes Pam almost walked into? They have to be the biggest Poison Ivy plants I have ever seen."

Mrs. Scott looks closely, "Terry, you're right. I'm used to it growing only as knee-high plants. I didn't give those green tree-size bushes a thought. If Pam or anyone else had walked into that patch, they would never have been able to finish the trip."

Mrs. Scott moves to Pam as she steps onto the grass. "Did you touch any of it?"

"I don't think so. Terry screamed just as I was reaching for it. I know what Poison Ivy looks like, but it didn't even register at all. Do I ever feel dumb!"

All the girls and staff have now gathered in a close group behind me and Mrs. Scott. Alison's comment follows in the next breath after Pam's. "Pam, welcome to my `dumb' club."

Mrs. Scott is quick to intercede, "We're not starting any `dumb' club, but today does seem to be a learning day. I'm afraid I would have done the same thing Pam was about to do. Terry pulled us out of a good one here. All of you look closely at this monster plant; I'm sure we'll see it again. After you've finished your look but no touch, eat your lunch, and we'll get back on the trail again."

As the group crowds to see the "leaves of three, let them be", I back out of all the campers. Looking around for Pam, I can't see her anywhere in the group. My eyes go on a search growing wider and wider. Finally, I see her on a rock down by the stream. Her back is to the group, and I'm certain she is crying.

Even if I don't want Pam around, I feel a little sorry for her. It is hard to make that big of a mistake in front of everyone. I am relieved to see Rusty, Pam's UL, walk up behind her and put her arm around Pam's shoulder. I turn my eyes and attention back to my unit.

The rest of the day is uneventful. After eating lunch, we are on our way again. Most of our hiking is out of the water. The canyon is wider, and in most places, there are trails along the banks. We continually move back and forth across the stream as the trail switches sides of the canyon. At about three in the afternoon, we come upon another grassy oasis. Mrs. Scott announced that this is our destination for the first day.

Mrs. Scott pulls the four Unit Leaders together for a short meeting. When Dixie and Tracy return to us, Tracy announces, "Our unit will camp on the west side of this grassy field. Let's get our camp set up and dinner on its way. We need to show those Explorers how to camp."

As the girls are moving to pick up their gear, she adds one last comment, "And watch out for Poison Ivy!"

I set up Sandy's and my tent and then watch as the camp comes together. I am proud of what I see. The girls are well organized and know exactly what to do. Everyone does her part and wants to do extra.

I pitched our tent on the grassy area next to the rock wall. The whole camp gently slopes from our temporary home to the stream. Sandy joins me as I survey our campers hard at work. "Terry, I like where you put our tent. It's out of the way, yet we can still keep track of everything that's going on." Looking toward the opposite side of the grassy field, she goes on, "We can even compare our unit with the Explorers. From the looks of things, their kids have been learning as well as ours. Their camp looks good, and I think that I can even smell their dinner."

Our attention is brought back to our group when Dixie shouts, "Hey, you two observers, are you going to join us for dinner?"

I yell back, "We'll be right there."

As we open our packs for eating utensils, I proudly say to Sandy, "I can't believe we're ready to eat. Our unit's better than I thought they were, and I thought they were good."

Hurrying down the trail, Sandy jokingly says, "Don't let it go to your head."

Both units join for an evening campfire. We sit in a crowded circle around a fire pit filled with wood, but no burning fire. The National Forest policy in this area is to carry in your fuel and leave the natural wood for everyone to enjoy.

I whisper to Dixie, "This is okay. This pretend fire gives everyone the feeling we're really at a campfire meeting. At the same time, no one misses the fire because it's still hot out here."

Dixie whispers back, "Did you ever think you'd be in a place where you got cold in the middle of the day when it's over a hundred degrees, then be too warm when the sun goes down and the temperature drops?"

I think about it, laugh, and am about to answer back when everyone joins in round singing. Singing leads to a couple of campfire skits, then into the Native American legend of the North Star, and more instruction from Mrs. Scott, "Be sure you drink only purified water." The evening ends with mellow singing.

When the last song ends, I turn back to Dixie, "We've slowed down just long enough that my body feels like it's ready for bed."

Dixie replies, "Everyone's moving like a bed is the next stop. I think we'll have a quiet camp tonight. Aren't you doing your usual and putting the fire to bed?"

I call back over my shoulder as I head toward our tent, "I'm going to work on a new image. I'm going to beat everyone to bed tonight."

I arrive at the tent at the same time Sandy does. We both crawl in and get ready for bed with no talk. When we are both settled in our sleeping bags, Sandy says, "One day down. Dixie said that tomorrow is going to be more challenging than today. This is going to be quite a trip if each day is harder than the last."

Not wanting to get involved in a lengthy conversation, I roll my back to Sandy and say, "We've got good kids. Let's get some good sleep so we'll be ready for that good challenge."

I close my eyes, but sleep is still far away. My mind moves back over the events of the day. I picture postcards around every turn in the river. I relive Alison's dunking. I watch the girls re-pitch the model camp. My mind can't settle on any one scene, but one common thread keeps appearing, Pam and agitation. If we were keeping score, I guess we are even for the day. I'm trying my best to keep as much distance between us as possible, but somehow there isn't enough space to get far enough apart. I make up my mind to try harder to avoid her tomorrow.

Before the sun has cleared the canyon rim, we're back in the water making our way downstream. The Adventurers are the trailblazers today, but Tracy and Sandy are leading the trek; Dixie and I are bringing up the rear of our unit.

For about two hours we weave back and forth across the stream, finding the dry trail again and again. Then the canyon narrows and pushes us back into the water. The sides became sheer red walls, rising straight into the sun. The canyon becomes so narrow that I can touch one wall with my hand and the other with my walking stick. When I look up, it looks as if the rims on both sides of the canyon almost touch.

Again, the thought crosses my mind. What would we do in a flash flood? I can see the waterline of past floods, and a log with stream debris caught in a crack in the wall about twenty feet above my head. I am about to bring this up again with Dixie when she notices that the girls in front are stopping, and everyone is bunching into a group.

Dixie and I move to the front of the group. She says, "I see we've come to our challenge for the day."

Sandy tries to speak to Dixie alone, but everyone is gathered so closely we can all hear what she's saying. "If this is what you were talking about yesterday, it's a real challenge. There's a drop right in front of us and we can't feel the bottom anywhere. Do we fly or swim?"

Dixie is about to speak when Mrs. Scott makes her way through the girls to the front. "I wondered if this little gathering meant we've come to the `Box Narrows'. There's more water in here than we've had any other year we've been here. This ought to be interesting."

The Explorers have caught up with the trailblazing Adventurers, and all the leaders are now in front, studying the deep water.

Mrs. Scott finally speaks, "Every time we've come to the canyons, we've brought our blow-up inner tubes. It looks like we'll finally get a chance to see if they work."

She speaks directly to the ULs saying, "Take out your tubes and ropes."

She continues speaking to everyone, "This has always worked well in theory. Now we'll see if it works in practice. We simply tie a rope to an inflated tube and one person climbs aboard. They float down to where they can touch. Once you're across the hole, we'll pull the tube back up, attach your pack, and float it back down to you. It'll take us a while, but we should be able to get everyone over this deep hole safe and sound. Now, all we need is a daring, brave, courageous assistant unit leader to try it out."

All the AULs look at each other, but no one speaks. Then one of the girls in the Explorers calls out, "Pam, you do it!"

Another shouts, "Pam can do it!"

I can see the Explorer girls are about to make the decision. Before anyone else can get on the bandwagon, I step forward a little, "I'll do it. What do I do?"

Dixie smiled as she says, "You'll make a good guinea pig. Put your pack on that rock over there and get ready for a ride."

I move over to the solitary rock at the side of the steep canyon wall and slipped off my pack. Dixie is just putting the finishing puffs into her tube as I make my way back to the front of the deep hole.

Dixie hands the tube and a rope end to me. "Tie that around the tube and climb aboard."

"Do I just lie down on the tube?"

"Sit in it like you were floating down one of the canals at home."

I feel uneasy about this adventure, but I try my best to look calm and cool. I am about to sit down when I ask one more question. "How will I know when I can touch the bottom?"

Dixie answers, "I keep forgetting you haven't been here before. The hole is only about ten feet wide. It drops off like you're stepping into a box and stays level until you reach the other side of the box. When we were here before, we walked through it. The water was about chest high. If we wanted to keep our packs completely dry, we had to carry them over our heads. Most of us were not that strong so we were glad everything inside was wrapped in plastic. Now you better get going before you chicken out."

That is all Dixie needs to say. I climb into my sailing position and start downstream as Dixie feeds out the rope. The whole group watches soundlessly and breathlessly. I drift lazily across the hole.

By the time I have gone about fifteen feet, I have relaxed completely. I yell back to the group, "I like hiking this way. I think we should go all the way down the stream on a tube."

I have hardly gotten the last word out when an explosion echoes in the canyon. It sounds like a gunshot. In the next instant, I disappear under the surface. A second later I shoot back up standing in waist-deep water.

I yell back to the group, "Did you fix that tube so it would pop? I thought for sure I was dead."

Seeing I am okay, the group relaxes and begins to laugh. When they quiet down Dixie calls back. "You're not the only one who thought you were dead. What did you run into?"

I feel around under the water and pull up a tree limb. The deflated tube is still attached to a sharp-pointed branch. I hold up the limb and yell at the group, "I'll bet you planted this here just so I'd get wet."

The group laughs again as the tension began to ease.

Mrs. Scott takes over the situation, "Terry, since you do that so well, I think you'd better do it again. We'll float you down another tube. This time tie the rope around your waist instead of the tube. We'll pull you back up. Walk downstream a few steps while you're waiting for us."

I take three steps downstream, and the water level moves down to just below my knees. I call back, "You were right, the water's back to shallow." I move to the side of the canyon and look downstream. "Just around the bend, there's a lot of light. It looks like the canyon widens out again."

The new tube is waiting at the end of its long rope, and Dixie calls out, "Terry, stop your sightseeing and climb aboard your yacht. We all want to get over there."

I take the rope off the new tube and tied it around my waist. I sit down for the trip upstream. My whole unit wants to help, so the trip back is over before I even get settled. I am almost afraid they're going to pull me off the tube.

When I get back to the group, I stand and look at Mrs. Scott. "Do you want me to do it again?"

"Yes, only this time with your feet down through the hole. We need to know if there's more debris under the water that we can't see. Since you are experienced and wet, you seem the likely candidate."

I have apprehension this time as I slip the tube over my head and walk into the water. The bottom sinks from beneath my feet and I am floating downstream again. I move my legs in a searching pattern. I am feeling for anything which might be there but hoping I will find nothing. I know it gives me an almost panic feeling to touch things under the water I can't see. My hopes are fulfilled when my feet touch solid ground, and I again walk up to shallow water.

I tie the rope around the tube for it to be pulled back upstream and call, "Put my pack on the tube, and let's see if it rides better than I do. I think it would be best to tie the rope to the pack and not the tube. If it gets pitched, at least we can pull it out."

As they attach my pack to the tube, Alison calls out, "I hope you put everything in plastic like you're supposed to."

Dixie laughs at her mimic of me the day before.

I smile and call back, "You better believe I did. How could I not, when I had such a good teacher yesterday."

They are about to launch the pack when I call, "Tuck my walking stick on that load someplace."

When all the girls and gear from the Adventurers have been transported over the hole, Dixie turns to me, "Lead the way to the light you were talking about. Sounds like a good spot for lunch."

My unit is lined up behind me ready to leave. I turn to look at the group and at the same time look past them to the far side of the Box Narrows. The Explorers are just beginning to cross. Pam is their first sailor. I look at her and say to myself, at least so far today, I'm not in second place.

CHAPTER 8

I'm sitting on an overhang looking down at camp Big Spring and the small stream. I'm on one of my early morning adventures and have climbed halfway up the side of the canyon to find this perfect spot. The air is still cool. The girls will not be up for at least a half-hour, and the sun will not spill onto the canyon floor for at least two hours. I love this time of day. My head always seemed clearer, and it feels exciting to be alive.

My eyes stare at the scene below, but I see only glimpses of the past week in my mind. It doesn't seem possible we've been in the canyon a whole week. Every day has been full to the brim, yet it seems like only yesterday we turned up this side canyon to Big Spring. I remember my thoughts as we set up camp on that day. The spring has plenty of water, and the scenery is gorgeous, but I can't imagine what we're going to do for two weeks.

I smile at my lack of vision as I think about what we have done.

We've visited Moky Indian ruins, adopted a swimming pool up Color Canyon at the base of the falls, and explored unnumbered side canyons. One week left, what could we possibly do that we haven't done? Here I am being a skeptic again. I should just trust the week ahead will be as exciting as the past week has been. I haven't seen Pam much, but still, my empty loneliness mixed with agitation and anger is growing. Increasingly the activities and excitement don't mask my feelings inside. I almost say aloud, "I wish there were a God to pray to. At least then I could talk to someone about what's happening to me." I catch myself and switch my thoughts back to camping.

Anyway, I am looking forward to tomorrow. Sandy and I will be hiking down the mainstream to pick up next week's fuel supply. It will be an all-day adventure, and I am looking forward to spending a relaxing time with her. I'm ready for a break from the girls. Even though the two units have gone their different directions during the day this past week, I have put every minute I had into being with my campers. Pam and I have been in two different worlds except for our evening campfires, and I like that arrangement.

I'm drawn out of my trance by shouts from the camp below. "Terry, you're going to be disqualified from the pancake flipping contest if you're not down in five minutes." I have let my time get away from me.

I am on my way down when I yell back, "If you think you're going to take away my title by flipping without me, you better think again."

Dixie hands me a frying pan as I fly into the cooking circle. "You must have fallen asleep up there. Everyone's through eating except you and Alison. She's been feeding everyone so she could practice. She's sure she can beat you this morning."

I am laughing inside because this is the fifth morning in a row that Alison has tried to beat me. Despite the inner laughing, I put on a business-like expression and say, "I'm ready for the contest. Who is my challenger this morning? Alison, it seems like we've met before."

Everyone laughs as they gathered for this morning ritual. "I've been practicing, and this morning I'm going to beat you, Terry."

I can't hold my smile back any longer, "Okay, you're first."

I continue, "Nicki, you're the official judge. Stand right in front of us on that rock and hold up the measuring stick. We're after the highest, with the most turns, landing brown-side up. Flip away, Ali."

As Alison loosens her pancake for the flip, she says, "This is a winner, Terry. I can feel it." She shakes the pan to make sure the pancake is loose and turns from the stove to Nicki. With an upward swing and a flick of the wrist, her cake goes up in the air, turns one and one-half times, and lands square in the pan brown-side up. Claps and cheers go up from everyone.

I am just putting the finishing touches on my cake and getting ready to flip when Dixie says, "Really good Ali. Terry, the pressure's on. I haven't seen you flip a two-and-a-half for a long time."

I want to make comments back, but I know that if I wait any longer, my cake will be too done. I hold my breath and turn to face Nicki. With a deep swing and a hard flip, the cake goes up in the air, turns two and a half times, and lands brown-side up.

Yells and shouts erupt from the group. When it quiets a little, Alison says, "How did you do that? I've never seen you do that before." Then with a look of total determination, she says, "I'm going to beat you if it's the last thing I do."

I think to myself, that was pure luck. It's been two years since I made one of those work. Then I remember why I haven't flipped since then. I had gotten sick eating all my mistakes.

To Alison I taunt, "It's just a matter of skill. Just remember the other rule. You can practice all you want, but you have to eat every pancake you flip."

I am about to protest that Alison isn't eating her practice cakes when we hear Mrs. Scott's call to the morning meeting.

"You two can clean up your mess after the meeting. We were the last ones there yesterday, but we're not going to be today." Dixie makes sure that every Adventurer is moving toward the meeting spot.

It appears neither unit wants to be tagged straggler, as everyone arrives at about the same time. Mrs. Scott is at her usual perch standing on a large rock. "You get speedier every morning. You all must be excited to get on with the day's activities. Since you're all ready to go, let's make this meeting short. Rusty, where are you taking the Explorers today?"

"We're going to 'The' swimming pool up Color Canyon."

Kristi, who's standing right behind me, yells at the whole Explorer group, "They better take good care of our pool."

Mrs. Scott looks down at Kristi and says, "I'm sure they'll treat it just as if it was their own."

When the Explorers have finished making comments, Mrs. Scott goes on, "Dixie, where are you taking your group today?"

"We're going into Slide Canyon. There's a flint out-cropping there. I think we'll learn how to pressure flake arrowheads."

"Sounds like a full day. Be careful and have fun. One more thing, tomorrow each unit will be short one staff. Terry and Pam will be going downstream to bring back the fuel supply. It'll be a long, all-day trip, so you both need to be ready to go with the first gray light of the morning."

As everyone starts back to their camp, I move straight to Dixie. Trying not to show the total frustration I feel inside. I say, "I thought Sandy and I were going down the canyon tomorrow?"

Dixie looks strangely at me, "We've talked about you going, but I never remember talking about Sandy. I just assumed you knew it would be someone from the other unit."

I realize that I must not be covering my disappointment very well when Dixie goes on, "If that's a problem, you'll have to talk to Mrs. Scott. She made the assignments, and she's the only one who can change them."

I watch Dixie turn and move quickly to catch up with the girls from our unit. Why is this happening? I have been so excited about tomorrow, and now I feel like screaming. I pick up a rock and throw it as far up the canyon wall as I can. I throw another and another, but nothing releases the emotions building inside. I know I need to be getting down to my unit, but I don't know how to handle the tears that are coming closer and closer. I move slowly in the direction of our camp, wondering how I will ever make it through this day. If I do make it through this day, how will I ever spend an entire day with Pam? I kick rocks as I fight for control of my anger. Dixie's words echo back through my mind, "You'll have to talk to Mrs. Scott. She made the assignments, and she's the only one who can change them." Maybe that's the answer. I'll talk to her when we get back from our arrowhead-making expedition. With that little ray of hope, I pick up my step to join my group.

I get to our tent just as Sandy is coming out with her hiking gear. From her hands and knees, she looks up at me, "You'd better get moving. We're about to leave without you."

Once she is standing, she continues, "I'm sorry about tomorrow. I was looking forward to getting away. I enjoy the kids, but it would have been fun to just be on our own for a day."

"Don't give up the ship yet. I'm going to talk to Mrs. Scott when we get back from the hike. There must be some way to change her mind."

"I wish you luck. That sounded like a final decision to me," Sandy says.

Our conversation is cut short by a shout from the whole group. "Let's go!" They are all waiting down by the stream and want to leave.

I duck into the tent. Sandy calls back over her shoulder as she moves toward the inpatient group, "Hurry, Terry. I'll stall them until you get there."

I am ready to go. I just need to grab my day pack and walking stick.

As I walk up the side of the hill to Mrs. Scott's hidden campsite, I realize I haven't been much of a leader this day. I talked very little with the girls. When they tried to joke with me, I had no comebacks or even a smile. Everyone seemed to have taken the hint and mostly left me alone. I rehearsed all day in my mind what I could say that would change Mrs. Scott's mind. Now the time is here none of my arguments feel good. When I am almost to the rock cluster that contains the director's tent, I debate about turning back. I stop and turn around and then think to myself. Why am I such a chicken? I don't have anything to lose by just talking to her. There's always a possibility she'll change her mind.

I whirl back around, take half a dozen steps, and call out, "Knock, knock. Is anybody home?"

A familiar voice calls back. "Come in, Terry. I've been expecting you."

I round the rock gate to find Mrs. Scott sitting on a flat rock writing in a notebook.

Her invitation to enter is my immediate opening for a conversation, "Why have you been expecting me?"

"Pam just left, and I assume that you're here for the same reason. You don't want to spend the day with her tomorrow."

I'm taken totally by surprise and hesitate as I answer, "Well, something like that."

"I'll tell you the same thing I told Pam. We chose the two most capable people in the camp to go down the canyon. You and Pam are the most skilled outdoor leaders on our staff, even if you are only AULs and JLs. It also doesn't make sense to take two people out of the same unit and leave one short-staffed. If you really can't tolerate each other for twelve hours, you'll both say here, and I'll send Dixie and Rusty. If you stay here, don't look for a permanent staffing position next summer" After a short pause, she adds, "What do you want to do?"

Looking at the serious expression on Mrs. Scott's face, I realize my whole future as a staff member at Lightning Mountain rests on what I say next. I choose my words carefully, "It's no big thing. Sandy and I have worked hard together. We just thought it would be fun to spend the day together. I'll do whatever you think is best for the camp."

Mrs. Scott's reply is crisp and to the point. "Good! Be ready to go first thing in the morning."

I turn to go, hesitate, and turn back. Mrs. Scott looks at me questioningly, "Is there something else, Terry?"

I look down as I ask her my question, "What did Pam decide?"

"The same thing you did. She'll be ready to go at dawn."

I turn and leave without another word.

It's still dark as I find a rock beside the stream to wait. I can't sleep any longer, so I decide to get ready and wait by the stream. As I stretch out on my back to wait, I mentally go through a check-off. In my pack, I have my first aid kit, lunch, filled water bottle, small survival kit, empty fuel cans, and a flashlight. I feel the pocket of my safari shorts to make sure I have transferred my pocketknife and lip balm when I changed pants. I also feel my nine-inch survival knife in its sheath belted around my waist and tied to my leg. My 104 is hanging out of my back pocket. I can't think of anything I've left behind, so I close my eyes to relax and wait.

I'm startled when I hear Mrs. Scott's voice right beside me. "That's one way not to be late, sleeping right here."

I realize I have fallen asleep, when I look around the sky is gray instead of black, and Pam is standing by Mrs. Scott looking down at me. I try to come back with a quick answer, "I just thought I'd rest a little while I waited."

Pam doesn't seem interested, and Mrs. Scott changes the subject almost before I finish speaking. "I'm glad to see you're both ready. You do look a little silly though, with shorts for the water, long-sleeved shirts for this chilly morning air, hats for the coming sun, and empty packs. This desert life causes people to do strange things."

I force a little laugh. It sounds as if Pam does the same thing, but neither of us says anything.

Mrs. Scott's voice takes on a more serious tone. "Just follow this stream down to the main canyon and turn right. It's about five miles to the parking lot. If you're following the water downstream, you'll eventually come to the trail's end and find the cars. Coming back will be more of a challenge. The car key is behind the left rear tire up under the car. You two have a fun time and please take care of each other."

Without looking at Pam, I pick up my walking stick and step into the water. The stream is wide and shallow. The gravel-sized rocks on the bottom make it easy to move. I set a moderate pace for Pam to follow, but I am surprised to find her crowding on my heels. As the space between us stays uncomfortably close, I turn to Pam, "What's the big hurry? We've got all day."

Without stopping, Pam growls, "There are a lot more things I'd sooner be doing than hiking back to the cars for extra fuel cans. I'd like to just get this chore over."

My heart sinks as I think to myself. This is going to be a worse day than I ever imagined. I decide I can play the same game. I stop and turn to face her. The tone in my voice changes to defiance, "If that's the way you want it, I'll make sure we get this trip over with, in a hurry."

I start back downstream again and double the pace. I'm angry at Pam and life in general. It isn't fair the way Pam and I are always ending up together. I didn't want to start the day off like this, but if that's what Pam wants, I'll give her more than she ever bargained for. I'll make this a day Pam will never forget. The only logical thing to do now is to get this trek over as soon as possible.

I push my body harder than I ever remember. My total concentration is on the water and looking for sure footing. My eyes stay glued down on my feet. All I let myself think about is push, push. At times I slacken my concentration while listening for Pam. She is still there about six feet behind. I do notice that the stream is picking up more water. The canyon is also getting wider, so the water depth stays about ankle deep. As we round a bend to my total amazement, we are at the parking lot. I stare at my watch and back at the cars. It has taken us only about two and one-half hours. I can't believe we are here. I also can't believe we have not said one word to each other the whole trip.

By the time we get to the camp vehicles, in addition to being exhausted, I'm feeling angrier than ever about this day. I'm lost in thought when Pam breaks the silence. "That was a record trip. Maybe we should eat our lunch before we start back."

I can tell that Pam is trying to melt the ice, but I can't let go of the feelings I have been building with every step down the trail. "It's not even nine o'clock yet, and I'm not hungry." I look straight at Pam, "Let's just get these cans loaded so we can get back to camp and do something we like to do."

When we're loaded up with the fuel, I glance at Pam. I am a little surprised that she doesn't even look tired. My mind moves back to the competition. She might be able to keep up with me, but there is no way she is going to outdo me. I'll stay ahead of her all the way back to camp if it kills me. We both move to the safety of silence and start back up the river.

With heavy packs, tired legs, and uphill hiking, our pace is cut to one-fourth the downstream speed. Our silence continues. About fifteen minutes up the river, I back up to a large rock, balanced my pack, and slipped out of my long-sleeved shirt. As I tie the sleeves around my waist while still balancing my pack, I comment, "It's too hot for sleeves." Although Pam says nothing, she follows in my example also taking off her shirt. With our outer layer shed, we again trudge up the stream in a communication blackout.

After about two hours, we come to a break in the canyon wall that opens out into one of those little grassy meadows. Even with no verbal agreement, we both head straight for the lush inviting grass and peel out of our packs. I collapse immediately on the green mattress and close my eyes to completely relax. I lay motionless for fifteen minutes waiting for energy to return to my body. When I finally opened my eyes, Pam is on the other side of the small meadow eating her lunch. As I sit up and open my pack for lunch, I wish with all my heart this war had not started today, but at this point, I don't know what to do with it.

Sitting on the grass, I suddenly realize I have a devastating problem. Because of my turned-in, angry self-talk, I haven't paid the slightest attention to my surroundings. My mind registered nothing on the way down the canyon. Looking around, it's like I am seeing this place for the first time. When I have enough strength to push again, I stuff the remainder of my lunch and my water bottle back in my pack and wade back into the mocking stream. Pam follows right behind me, still in dead silence.

Towering four-hundred-foot walls on both sides flank us as we tramp uphill through the water. I am almost panicked that I can't even recognize one landmark. Every side canyon we pass could be our turn-off. We push against the oncoming current and the uphill grade for another two hours. I'm sure at times my watch has stopped. The strain of the hike mixed with the strain of the relationship makes it seem as if ten hours have passed instead of four. Using how I feel and the time on my watch as a distance indicator, I begin to look earnestly for our side canyon. I figure we must be close. As we pass three side canyons, I am disgusted with myself. I spent so much time being angry and pushing to top Pam that I'm lost. Nothing looks familiar. After passing two more side canyons, I realize that I don't know which canyon to turn up. They all look like the right one in some ways and in other ways they do not. When we come to the next side canyon opening on our left-hand side, I turn to go up.

Pam finally breaks the silence, "Terry, I don't think this is the right canyon." I can't handle making that big of a mistake in front of Pam, but at the same time, I'm not sure of the canyon myself. I venture cautiously, "Are you sure it's not the right one?" with lots of emphasis on the "sure".

"No! I'm not sure. I was so mad coming down I didn't pay attention to anything," Pam says.

Even though I have some doubts, I can't let Pam put me down, "I know this is the right canyon. You'll see. Fifteen minutes up this small stream, and we'll see our camp and Big Spring."

Pam still hesitates until I say, "If you don't think this is the right way, go find your own canyon."

Pam's look turns back to total ice, and her body turns to follow me up the questioning canyon.

We again walked in silence. At first, everything looks familiar and I know that we are going the right way. Gradually my confidence fades, and a nagging fear begins to take its place. We persist up the side canyon for a little less than an hour. I finally accept that I don't know where we are and brace myself for the angry onslaught of words, I know Pam's going to throw at me.

Pam shatters the silence, "Terry, this is not the right canyon! I don't think you—"

Her words are cloaked by a low roll of faraway thunder. Both of our heads snap up to see the distant mountains covered in angry black clouds. My mind swims in self-condemnation. Why have you not been paying attention to the canyon or the weather? Why!? My anxiety level is soaring.

Overhead, lightning splits an ominous thunderhead simultaneously as thunder explodes in a ground-shaking rumble.

Pam's next words exude sheer panic, "Terry, it's raining."

We gape up in horror as the rain begins pelting us from the massive cumulonimbus cloud over our heads. I'm beginning to visualize a gigantic flash flood racing down the canyon floor toward us. The look on Pam's face says she is imagining the same scene.

"We've got to get to high ground!" I scream as my mind finally starts functioning. I turn to throw off my pack and begin running downstream with Pam on my heels.

After splashing through knee-deep water for five minutes, we round the bend spotting the rockslide I hoped I'd remembered.

We begin climbing the slippery hunks of rock, scrambling for a ledge thirty feet above the canyon floor. Halfway up the rockslide, I put my hand on a large boulder to get leverage. Instead of giving me a boost up, the massive stone begins rolling back down the slide.

I yell, "Rock," and take a quick look back for Pam.

Pam's head jerks up. She quickly sidesteps allowing the hunk of sandstone to pass inches from her leg. We both watch as the five-foot diameter rock splashes into the swelling, angry river and disappears. Struggling again, we both move tripping and falling up the rest of the jumbled mass of boulders.

Finally, the ledge is at my eye level. I put my hands on the outcropping and jump with all my adrenalin. I raise in the air but hang short of my goal; I can't get my upper body over the edge of the shelf. In that instant, I feel a hard shove from below. With Pam's push, I get onto the ridge.

I quickly turn and catch hold of Pam's arm as she is trying the same strength maneuver. Pam is starting to get onto the ledge when a sound like Niagara Falls explodes in the air. A wall of water at eye level is ripping down the canyon coming around the bend. I instantly drop flat wrapping my arms around Pam's back under her arms. I lock my right hand on my left wrist, and Pam grabs me as tightly as she can. We are both screaming when the flash flood hits.

CHAPTER 9

The flood strikes covering both of us. After the initial surge passes, our heads are mostly above water. We cough and sputter as waves splash our faces, but we can at least get enough air to breathe between splatters.

Most of Pam's body is still in the racing current, and the force begins pulling us slowly down the ridge. My anxiety skyrockets—I can see we are being pulled down the narrowing ledge to be dumped into the snarling torrent.

"Father, please help us!" I begin praying with more sincerity than I have ever prayed before. My prayer is continuous, non-stop pleading from the bottom of my soul. Our sliding stops, but the power of the pushing water does not. Then a peaceful calm engulfs me. I know my petition to heaven has been heard. I can feel we are being held in place by invisible hands.

My plea changes as my voice raises upward again., "Father, please give me the strength to get Pam out of the river onto this shelf."

While I had been fiercely holding onto Pam in the water, I had felt a sharp burning pain in my left arm for an instant, but then thought no more about it. Slowly the initial force of the flood begins to dissipate. I pull with new power, and gradually Pam inches her way up onto the ridge. When she is completely on the ledge, we both scoot backward on the sloshing ground away from the roaring river. We move all the way to the wall which has an overhang that shelters us partially from the rain.

Once away from the rushing water, we stare at the raging torrent that could have been our grave. I begin to realize how close we came to being at the bottom of the canyon when that wall of water hit. Judging from Pam's pallor, I decide that she is thinking the same thing.

Observing Pam getting whiter, I put my hand on her leg and try to yell above the roar of the water, "You better lay back! I think you're going to faint".

Pam doesn't seem to hear me, but my touch takes her gaze away from the river. She looks at me and is instantly on her feet reaching for my left arm. I follow Pam's actions with my eyes. My stomach turns over like it might be my turn to be sick or pass out instead of Pam. There is a gaping cut just below my elbow; I can see the white glistening bone shimmering in the light. Blood is also squirting from my wound in a pulsing arc making a puddle on the ground.

Pain finally pierces through my arm, and my head begins to swim in dark circles. Pam grabs my arm pulling the sides of the cut together and pushes her hand hard against the cut. All the time she works, she talks to me. "Something in the water must have hit your arm while you were hanging on to me. We've got to get that bleeding stopped. I hope I'm not hurting you too much."

I look down at my hemorrhaging arm and Pam in disbelief. "I remember feeling a hot flash on my arm, but that's all. Now that I know it's there, I'm being assaulted with stabbing pain. I think I'm going to be sick."

Still holding tight to my arm, Pam senses my weakness. "Lay back, Terry! You've lost a lot of blood. I don't know how you ever held on to me."

My head is spinning, but I try to concentrate on what Pam is saying instead of my cut. "It's lucky I gripped the way I did. I held on to that wrist. That arm didn't need any strength. It just needed to be there."

When the bleeding begins to slow down, Pam looks searchingly into my eyes, "Your bleeding is almost stopped. I think I can fix you up with a better bandage than my hand. Do you still have your 104?"

I am now holding my left arm in excruciating pain. "Look in my back pocket."

Pam quickly pulls the large handkerchief from my back pocket and begins to make a fast dressing and bandages. She rips five one-inch strips from one edge with her teeth and one hand and then folds the remaining piece to make a dressing which she places directly on the oozing slash. She never lets go of my wound with her other hand which is still applying direct pressure until she applies the dressing. The bandaging strips are quickly applied to the dressing tight enough to hold everything secure and continue putting pressure to control bleeding. Pam takes her wet handkerchief, folds it into a triangle, and places my injured arm in a sling.

I look at Pam with new eyes, "You really are a doctor You've saved my life twice in the last fifteen minutes. First, you push me up on this ledge, and then you keep me from bleeding to death."

When everything is in place, Pam leans back in her kneeling position looking strangely at me, "I volunteer as a paramedic in the emergency room two days a week. To help there, I had to take advanced first aid and paramedic EMT classes. As to saving lives—I wouldn't be here if you hadn't held on to me when that watery wall hit. I prayed the flood wouldn't rip me out of your arms. I will never be able to repay you for your strength and courage."

"Pam, I give all the credit for saving both our lives to unseen powers from heaven. An outside force was holding onto us. Without that extra help, we'd both be racing downstream, underwater, dashing into rocks." Pam is quiet just staring at me as she contemplates our rescue. She then gently places her hand on my injured arm, "Terry, when you do something, you do it all the way. It's cut down to the bone, and I think you've severed all the tendons on the top of your arm. Can you open your hand?"

I peer down at my clenched fist. Try as I will, I cannot make my fingers move. My efforts only succeed in bringing pain that almost causes me to blackout. I shake my head to answer no.

Pam gently takes hold of my hand and slowly unclenches my fingers. She then pokes them with a little sharp-pointed stick and asks me what I feel. I ask her if she is trying to make me into a pincushion.

I see a faint smile on Pam's face as she speaks, "You don't know how good this is. You still have feelings in your fingers. All the cut muscles and tendons in your arm can be repaired, but if you had severed your nerve, you would never be able to use your hand again. As soon as we get out of here, you'll need to be stitched back together. But for now, we'll just keep it quiet and try to keep down the pain—I can't believe you held on to me with that cut."

I close my eyes against the horror of losing the use of my hand and the throbbing pain. "Terry, open your eyes long enough to take these pain pills and drink this water," Pam speaks softly. "We'll work on your shock and pain at the same time."

I stare at the tablets and the water bottle in Pam's hands in amazement. "Where did you get these? Did you bring your pack up here?"

"Terry don't be silly. I did well to get myself up here with your help. When we stopped to eat, I had a doozy of a migraine. I had prescription pain pills in my pack for just such a problem. With the way our day was going, I decided to put my little waterproof pill box in my pocket in case my headache got worse. I also strapped my water bottle to my belt so I wouldn't have to get in my pack. Take the pills, drink up, and rest while I go exploring.

Pam stands and looks around at our next challenge. Her last comment is, "Don't move your arm!"

All I want to do is sleep. I have never felt so weak. My eyes are closing as Pam walks out from the overhang which is sheltering us from the sprinkling rain.

"Terry, wake up for a little," Pam says as he touches my shoulder. "I have to tell you what I found." I shake off the grogginess and try to focus on Pam. "This place is fantastic. You'd never know from the bottom of the canyon there's a little oasis here. We have a big two-acre meadow on the other side of those boulders." Pam says as she points to the stone mounds in front of us. "At the back of the grassy area by the canyon wall, there're huge cottonwood trees, willows, and cattails. I think we're in a perfect spot, and I'm sure we're going to be here for a few days. We do, however, have one giant problem—I know nothing about survival. I couldn't even find water in the place where cattails are growing."

I groan a deep anguished moan.

"Terry, do you have more pain? I didn't even see you move."

"Pam, this is a vastly different kind of pain. Since I was a little girl, I have gone on camping and survival trips with my family. When my parents died, my brother continued the tradition. It's our recreation to spend a couple of weeks living off the land every summer. I was always told that someday it might save my life. Now my life hangs on survival skills, and I can't move. I am so weak I can't even get up off the ground.

Pam looks searchingly at me, "Terry, you may not be able to use your hands, but your mind still works. You still know what to do and how to do it. You are *"The"* survival expert. I have never had the chance to learn the skills you have. If you teach me, I will try being your hands. I could never be as good as you are, but together, we might make it."

I look into Pam's eyes and see her deep sincerity. I also realize how desperately I need her. I know I can't survive without her help, and she won't without mine. I must let go of my puffed-up pride and trust her. The only way we'll both live is if we selflessly work together.

After a long pause, I swallow, "Okay Pam, you be our hands." The words are hard to say, but they are honest.

"What's first?" Pam asks. I watch her visibly relax at the same time.

Still lying very still I say, "There's not much time left before dark. At this point, the two most important things we need are better shelter and a fire."

Pam says, "You rest some more, while I work on the shelter. There are enough rocks and cliffs around here, I should be able to find something just made for us.

Pam crawls out from under the overhang and stretches while getting her bearings. As she is looking around, I call out, "Can you see the river?"

"I can. It hasn't changed much. The water level has dropped about two feet but has about twenty-eight to go. It's not raining here anymore, but it looks like it's still pouring in the mountains. Relax, I'll be back in a while."

I close my eyes again and can feel the pain pills still working. As I drift off to sleep, I am glad for two things. Some of my emptiness is gone, and Pam and I are at least talking. To be in this mess and have ice between us would be impossible and dangerous.

"Terry, wake up! It's time to move to your new home."

"I thought you said that I should rest a while. I just barely got to sleep."

"That just barely was an hour and a half ago. Wait until you see what I found," Pam says enthusiastically.

"You found a secret passage back to Big Spring?" I ask jokingly.

"Well, it's not quite that great, but it is neat. About twenty-five yards along the wall from where we are, there's a cave. It's perfect for us. It's dry and goes back in far enough that it will be good protection. I even collected firewood. All I need now is to know how to build a fire. My waterproof match holder leaked, and my matches are so wet the ends dissolved. Do you have any dry ones?"

I feel my pocket and groan again. "They're in my pack, along with my flint and steel, and water bottle. The only survival equipment I have is my pocketknife and my survival knife."

"We make a good pair. My knife is in my pack. Can we start a fire without matches?"

I manage a little smile. "The very hardest part of survival is making a matchless fire. You would pick that for your first lesson."

Pam reaches out her hand to help me up. "First things first, we have to see if we can get you to our mansion."

"I thought you said that it was a cave?"

"It is. But compared to this place, it's a mansion. Move slowly and try not to move your arm."

I turn on my side and scoot out from the low overhang with Pam's help. It takes a long time to finally get me standing so the world doesn't look as if it is spinning like a run-away merry-go-round. I have my good arm on Pam's shoulder while she holds her arm around my waist. Together we slowly make our way through the rock maze toward the waiting cave. When we clear the rock barricade, I glance around the green paradise we have climbed into. This might not be too bad of a place to practice survival; I think as we shuffle along. It's just not right that I don't have two good hands to work with.

As we creep along, I can tell some of my strength is returning. I'm not going to win any races, but at the same time, I don't feel as if I'm going to faint with every step. When we finally make it to the cave, I look around approvingly. "Pam, you did well. This does look like a mansion."

We move inside to the wall by the cave entrance, and Pam helps me to sit down. "There's even a place for you to kind of sit and lay at the same time while you supervise this fire building," Pam points out.

I start Pam's instructions, "I think I'll be ready for you as soon as you find all the materials you need. Go back to the green area by the back wall of the meadow. Find a dead and dry piece of Cottonwood about two feet long and 1 to 2 inches wide. It needs to be at least a half-inch thick and long enough to put your foot on and drill at the same time." Pam looks at me with a confused lost look. "Drill, what are you talking about?"

"This is going to be interesting. I can tell," I say. "Don't worry about a drill, just get the wood. Besides the cottonwood, get two willows. One that's dead, about three-quarters of an inch in diameter and a foot long. The other should be green, about a half-inch in diameter, and two feet long. If you can get the green one with a little fork on one end, it would be good. You will also need a big pile of juniper bark. You can pull it off from those juniper trees on the hill by our cave." I clumsily unbuckle my survival knife, sheath, and all. "Belt on my survival knife and tie the bottom of the sheath around your thigh."

Pam stares at me in disbelief, "Terry, I have never even held a knife that big. What if I cut off my fingers?"

"I've watched you teach knife skills to all kinds of campers, Pam. You won't have any problem. Once you start using it, you'll want one of your own...Good luck. You'll have to hurry a little; we only have a little of the afternoon left."

Pam buckles on the knife and hurries toward the trees. She calls back over her shoulder, "You're right! This is going to be interesting."

I sit thinking about how to talk Pam through building a matchless fire and remember that she needs one more piece of wood. I look around and smile as I see a chunk of weather-beaten wood about an inch and a half thick and just big enough to fit in the palm of one's hand. I couldn't have found a better piece if I had gone looking for it. I close my eyes to wait for Pam.

I don't get to rest long when Pam rushes back into the cave with her arms full. "That didn't take long if I got the right stuff. Check this out Terry and tell me what's next."

I wake from my light sleep and look over Pam's treasures. "Looks good, I think you're ready to build a matchless fire. You've got enough juniper bark to make the spark bed as well as a real bed or at least pillows. Take some of the bark and rub it together until it shreds and makes a fine nest. The finer you can get it the better."

Pam rubs and scrubs the juniper bark between her two hands until she has a handful of powdery fine fibers. "That looks good. That's the bed for the spark. It must be as fine as you can make it. The first hard part is to get a spark. The second is to get the spark into the juniper bed and blow it into a flame. Most of the secret for starting a matchless fire is having a good tinder bed."

"I'm beginning to feel like a real Indian," Pam says.

"The Indians knew how to do this, but even they preferred to carry a fire bundle with a live coal than starting from nothing. Take the flat piece of cottonwood and carve a little depression on the flat top near the side." I point to a spot on the wood about an inch and a half from the edge.

Once that's done, I go on with the instructions. "Cut a notch from the outside edge to the center of the little pit you just carved. That notch catches the fine powder ground off by the drill, and that's where the spark grows."

"Terry, I still can't picture exactly what I'm doing, so if I don't do it right, let me know."

"Practice will be your best teacher as soon as we get you put together. Take the lace out of my hiking boot. Hook it to both ends of your green stick making a bow," I direct.

"The picture is getting clearer. Now, do I just put this other stick in the bow and turn? I've seen this part on TV." Pam excitedly explains.

"Not quite so fast. Round one end of that dead willow and carve a point on the other end. You have to have some way to hold it in place while it turns."

I point to the piece of wood I discovered. "Take that little piece of wood and carve a little hole in the center and put it on the point of your dead willow. That's how you hold on to the drill."

Pam chuckles, "When you said drill before, all I could think of was my father's big drill. I get the feeling that's not what you mean."

"The principle is the same. If your dad didn't have a sharp cutting edge on his drill bit, he would have a fire instead of a hole. Take that stick you just carved, lay it on the bowstring, and twist it around once so the string is wrapped around the stick. Put the blunt end into the depression on the board with the notch and hold the top of it with your little chunk of wood. Kneel on one knee so that you can put the other foot on the board that's on the ground and begin pulling that bow back and forth with the other hand."

As Pam fumbles trying to keep each piece of wood doing its job, she says, "This is kind of hard to make everything work at the same time. Are you sure it ever gets going fast enough to make a spark?"

A wave of tiredness sweeps over me. Speaking slowly, I say, "Keep working at it. It will finally come." My last words are barely distinguishable as I fall into an exhausted sleep again.

When I wake about two hours later it's almost dark, and I can't shake the dream I've been having. My mother has been talking to me. She says over and over, "Terry we're alright, but you're getting further and further away."

The aroma of juniper smoke brings me back to consciousness. I open my eyes to see a tiny flame Pam is desperately feeding with small twigs. I smile a little as I speak, "You did it. That's a record-breaking first-time fire. Most people are up half the night trying to start their first fire."

"It feels like I've been at it half the night. Terry, that's the hardest thing I have ever done. It takes an eternity to get a spark. When I finally got the spark into to tinder bed, I realized a spark and a flame are worlds apart. After I tried getting twenty sparks to flame, I stopped counting. I was ready to give up, but I just had to keep trying one more time. I can appreciate why the Native Americans carried their fire with them. You'll have to teach me how to do that another time." She looks intently at me and continues, "You sure must have been dreaming; you kept telling someone not to leave. How are you doing anyway?"

"I can't tell. I need to stretch my legs a little. This ground is getting harder by the second."

I start getting up and am glad Pam is right there to help me. "Once I'm up for a minute, I think I'll be a little steadier," I say.

"Terry, I'll just hold onto you until you can walk a straight line. Our fire is giving out quite a bit of light now, so you can have a little stroll. When you're finished exploring, we need to get the rest of the water in you."

I start walking away from the fire and turn back. "I think I'll have that drink right now. I'm dying of thirst."

"You can drink all of it except for a couple of swallows. You're going to need some more of those pain pills to make it through the night, and you'll need something to wash them down."

I drink as if I have been without water for a week but save the last half-inch for later. As I hand back the bottle, I say, "Thanks, you're a lifesaver."

Pam looks away from me as she takes back the bottle. "Don't thank me. You're the real lifesaver. I wouldn't be here at all if you hadn't hung on to me and pulled me up after that wall of water hit. Terry, I owe you, my life."

I don't know quite what to say so I mumble as I walk away from the fire, "Oh, but you pushed me up on the ledge to start with."

I make my way slowly toward the meadow, even my thoughts are shaky. I may have held on to Pam, but it was another force that saved our lives. If I am a hero, it's a short-lived glory for right now I can't even walk twenty-five feet without feeling exhausted. The more I walk, the more my arm hurts, and the more I just want to lie down on the ground and go back to sleep. Deciding I had better go back, I turn and head for the bright firelight. I stop just before entering the cave and look up to see if the moon is out. A drop of rain splashes me in the face. I am more thankful than ever Pam found this shelter for the night.

Pam looks up from the pile of bark as I make my way around the fire and into the cave. "Welcome back to the mansion. I decided to take you at your word about the bark bed. I've been scrubbing up this juniper bark, but I think I only have enough for small pillows. If we're here tomorrow, I'll work on the bed."

I can feel the warmth the fire is pushing from the cave. It's built just far enough in that the rain can't get to it, but at the same time the smoke is being pulled into the cool, wet, night air. I move toward Pam, "You were right about needing those pills. My arm's starting to hurt like crazy. Pam, I'm sorry that I can't help."

"Don't worry about anything but trying to get through the night. Here are your pills. I wish we had more water for you right now."

"I'll survive. We'll find some first thing in the morning." Looking down by the fire I hesitate, then say, "Take those little rocks, and put them in the fire."

Pam looks at me questioningly and picks up some small pebbles. "Do you mean these?"

I shake my head, "No, the ones over a little further which are about an inch in diameter." I watch as Pam moves her hands to the stones, "They're the ones. Just put them in the fire. Kind of put them on the edge but far enough in so that it's really hot."

"They'll be red hot in about five minutes in this fire. Terry, what are you going to do with them?"

Going on without seeming to answer her question, I ask, "Pam do you think you can get back to the stream and get some water without getting lost or falling in?"

"Sure, it's not very far." She hesitates as she starts into the night with the water bottle, "I think that water will make us sick without some kind of purification."

"You get the water, and I'll work on the germ-free part," I mumble.

It seemed like less than two minutes until Pam is back with a bottle full of muddy water. "Okay, Miss. Wizard, do your stuff. Out and back, I tried to figure out how you were going to make this clean enough to drink. You can't put the bottle in the fire to boil it because it's made of plastic. You don't have any purification tablets or a filter, and we don't have anything to put it in to boil. How are you going to do this?"

I love the riddles of survival. I only wish I had two capable hands to show Pam instead of just telling her what to do. I resign myself to being the teacher. "Take the stick you used for a bow to start the fire and cut each end flat, so they look like little paddles. Bend the stick until the ends are about three inches apart. Use my shoelace again and tie it about eight inches up so that the ends can't flip apart."

"This looks like a giant extra-long bobby pin with a tie in the middle. Keep talking. I'm still guessing," Pam says.

"Please make sure my lace doesn't hang down and get burned while you use your tongs to take those hot rocks out of the fire. Put one rock at a time into your water bottle."

The light dawns in Pam's eyes. "I get it. If you can't take water to the fire, you take fire to the water." As Pam puts each fiery ingot into the bottle, the water grows hotter. When she drops in the fourth, the water boils.

As tired as I am, I beam with delight. "It will still be kind of muddy when it cools down, but at least we'll have a little drinkable water by morning." Now I am beyond exhaustion again. "Where's my pillow? I thought I'd had enough sleep to last for the night, but now I feel like I could sleep for a week."

"Your pillow's right here." Handing me my juniper pillow and pointing to the ground, she goes on. "This area seems to be the warmest and most shaped like a bed. Crawl in. I'll try putting enough wood on the fire to keep us warm through the night."

I melt onto the designated spot and am asleep before my body starts complaining about the hard ground. Pam stokes up the fire with large pieces that will burn for hours and is almost asleep before her head hits her bark pillow.

About three o'clock in the morning, we are both brought to our full senses by the snarl and scream of an adult cougar at the entrance of our cave.

CHAPTER 10

The angry animal snarls again, and both of us sit up straight. My quick hurried movements bring fiery shooting pains through my whole side. I fight lightheadedness as I try to get a grip on the situation. Despite the pain and the whirling cave, I manage to get out two words, "The fire!"

Pam is in a trance as she stares into the glowing eyes across the dying fire. My words break the spell and send her into action. She reaches down for her bark pillow and throws it on the bed of coals. The shredded bark jumps instantly into flame. Then she quickly reaches for wood from the pile to feed the new flames. She puts small limbs on at first to catch fire quickly and continues adding larger and larger pieces until the fire is a roaring wall between us and the cougar. The animal backs up to escape the heat but does not leave. He continues his growling protests.

Seeing that Pam is well on top of the situation, I lay back against the wall to see if I can get the pain to quiet down. When Pam has the fire roaring and is contemplating what to do next, I speak. "I think someone else claims this as his mansion. We have moved into that cougar's bedroom, and he's not too happy. It's a good thing he's not a mother coming to feed her cubs in the back of this cave. Even the fire wouldn't have stopped her."

Pam can hardly get out the words, "He still doesn't sound too stopped. He sounds mad. I can even hear him breathing out there."

I know I am as scared as Pam sounds, but I try to keep a calm tone in my voice. I also know we will be in big trouble if either of us panics. "Pam, somehow he just needs a little more encouragement to find another home for a few days. We must have been as much of a surprise to him as he is to us."

"If you think that's what he needs, we'll give him all the help we can." She points to the ground, "Hand me your pillow."

When I hand Pam my shredded bark headrest, I half-jokingly ask, "Are you going to make him a bed outside?"

Pam takes the ball of bark and tosses it onto the fire. Instantly it is in flames. At the same time it ignites, Pam reaches two long sticks under the flaming pillow and flicks the fireball out of the fire in the direction of the waiting mountain lion. The attack catches the cat by surprise as the fiery mass lands on his front paws. He screams and dashes away into the black night.

Sitting back down, Pam watches the empty spot on the other side of the fire for a long time. "I don't think my heart will ever leave my throat or beat slowly again. I thought for a second he was coming in here," Pam says.

I continue trying to calm the situation, "I think he thought about it too. That was good thinking on your part. You've taken this fire-building stuff to a new level."

"When I was looking into those glowing eyes just across the fire pit, and you said 'Fire,' all I could think about was trying to blow those hundreds of sparks into a flame. Then the big piles of bark I made for our pillows flashed into my mind. After that, I hardly remember thinking of anything except making the fire big. Do you think he'll come back?"

I try to reassure both of us, "I don't think he'd dare. That flying ball of fire you sent him should keep him pretty leery of this place for some time." I continue a little slower and a lot softer. "That was super good thinking. You saved both of our lives with your quick work."

Without shifting her gaze away from the fire, Pam mumbles, "I guess that makes us even."

Not feeling comfortable with where the conversation is heading, and not wanting to create any communication problems, I quickly changed the subject. "Let's try some of that water you brewed up before we went to sleep. It ought to be cool enough to drink now."

Pam retrieves the water bottle and hands it to me. I shake my head, "You're first this time. Hold the bottle as still as possible. Most of the dirt has settled to the bottom."

Pam pulls the bottle back and takes off the lid. She looks hard at its contents and then at me. "It's a good thing we only have firelight to look at this stuff. Are you sure it's safe?"

"It may not taste the best, but it's safe. It'll tide us over until we have some light to find clear, clean water."

Pam puts the container to her lips and takes a little sip. She swallows it and waits. She then tips the bottle back up and drinks about a fourth of the contents in one breath. When she comes up for air, she says, "It's not too bad if you drink it fast. That way, you only have to taste it once when you're through." Handing the bottle to me she says, "The rest is yours."

I take the bottle, look inside, and say to myself, it does look gross, but I'm dying of thirst. I close my eyes and gently started drinking. Pam does have the right idea, drink without stopping to taste.

While I'm in the middle of my long drink, Pam stops me. "Terry, you'd better save a little for some pills. I don't imagine your arm feels too good after our little excitement."

I slowly lower the bottle to avoid churning up the junk. "You're right. It's killing me. When we sat up with that first snarl, I thought I was going to die twice, once from the cougar and once from the pain. With the cougar gone, my heart has calmed down a little, but my arm still thinks it's at war."

Pam pulls out the little plastic box from her pocket and investigates it by the firelight. "There are six pills left. If you take two now, there ought to be enough left to help you through tomorrow. I don't think you'll need as many painkillers during the day as you do at night. Do you think we'll get out of here tomorrow? How long will it take the water to go down?"

As I take the pills, I answer all the questions in one sentence. "Thanks. I don't know. I don't know." We both laughed a little as we try to shake loose from the tension. "I don't know. If it would stop raining in the mountains which feed this little stream, we could be on our way out by tomorrow night. Since it's still raining, your guess is as good as mine. We can't get out, and no one can get in. I wonder if everyone's given us up for total goners."

"We've come close twice, but we're far from being gone," Pam says. "I hope everyone in the camp made it to high ground. Terry, you better get some more rest. I have a feeling you're going to be teaching many more survival lessons tomorrow."

I can feel the pills are starting to help and look at the ground for a sleeping spot. I try a couple of places and am about to shift to a third when Pam says "Since I took your pillow, why don't you put your head on my lap? I'm just going to lean back against the wall right here so I can feed this fire. I doubt if I'll sleep much. I don't think I trust our overgrown feline friend. If I were out in that rain, I'd want my dry home back." I take Pam up on her offer and am asleep before she has even added the first stick to the fire.

When I wake, it's to my early morning alarm and a stab of pain. I look around without moving. The fire is a large bed of slow-burning coals and not putting out much heat. From the size of the woodpile, I can tell Pam has fed it several times while I slept. I figure she must have finally gotten so tired her fatigue overcame the fear of the returning cougar. She is now half lying, half sitting back against the wall of the cave, sound asleep. I lay looking out at the early morning sky; I see streaks of bright orange everywhere. I think colored clouds in the morning are not a good sign. I wonder what this day will hold. I also think about how good it feels not to be in pain and a little rested. I still don't dare move much. Closing my eyes, I drift back into a light sleep.

I wake quickly when Pam moves to put more wood on the fire. I don't even lift my head from her lap, "Thanks for getting us through the night. Did you get any sleep while keeping watch for the former proprietor?"

"More than I thought I would. It was still dark when I remember putting the last wood on the fire. It's light now, and the fire's almost out. Sometime, I closed my eyes. I don't think you ever woke up, even when I was putting wood on the fire. How do you feel?"

"I don't have much pain, but I don't dare move. I even feel a little rested thanks to you providing a heavenly pillow. I'll bet you don't feel too rested. I'll see if I can get up, so you can at least change your position. Your ground must feel like cement; mine does."

Pam helps me to a sitting position. "Go slow and try not to move your arm. How do you feel sitting up?"

"Like laying back down. I think I'll be okay if I sit here for a minute." The world feels a little tipsy, but I am thankful the pain is still minimal.

"I'm not going to let this fire go out if I have to babysit it all day," Pam says while she's adding wood to the fire. That duty discharged; she goes outside into the morning sun.

"Terry, it's beautiful out here. You ought to see the sky. I've never seen so much color in a sunrise. I am also hungry enough to eat a horse."

With Pam's help, I finally make it to my feet and slowly walk around the fire to stand outside. "I wish this beauty suggested good things. Remember the old weather jingle, 'Red sails in the morning, sailors take warning. Red sails at night, sailors delight.' Those pretty clouds mean we have more storms coming. Before it gets here, we had better start working on your horse."

"I don't think I could eat a real horse even if we found one, but I'm sure hungry."

"We won't find any horses, but you may still have to break a mindset. What we find, may seem worse than a horse. First, we'll look at your spring. We better take the water bottle with us."

As Pam goes back into the cave for the bottle, she keeps the conversation going. "I'm counting on you having some sort of magic I don't have. I looked all over for water back there yesterday, and I couldn't find a drop. Do you think you can walk that far?"

With my good arm on Pam's shoulder and Pam's arm around my waist, we start across the meadow. "I don't know. I have a little more strength than I had yesterday. If I go slow and don't let my arm move, I think I'll be okay."

We walk very slowly with me setting the pace. After stopping several times, we finally walk into the lush green foliage at the base of the canyon wall. I go right to the thickest, richest green area and look at the ground. We walk around until I find a wet sandy area. "Pam, this is the place."

165

Pointing to a limb about three feet long and an inch and a half thick I say, "Bring that stick. It looks like a good digging stick. I'll just sit on this rock while you start digging right here."

"How do you dig a hole with a pointed stick? I need a shovel," Pam complains.

"Survival, Pam, you need to think survival. Push the pointed end into the ground, and then move the stick sidewise to loosen the dirt. When you get a bunch of ground loose, scrape it out with your hands. Make a hole about a foot and a half across and the same depth."

Pam attacks the ground with vengeance and works quickly. "This wet sand makes easy digging. I hope we find some water so I can wash some of this dirt off my hands."

When she has dug down about six inches, the fine sand gets coarser and mixes with more water. "This is exciting. The further down I dig, the wetter this sand gets. If this keeps up, we might find water."

Pam works until the hole is about two feet deep. She digs with the stick and then scoops with her hands time after time. The oozing mixture doesn't seem to change, but each handful holds promise there must be clear water, deeper. I watch her intently until I am satisfied. "That looks good for now. Let's go work on some food."

Pam looks at me and digs faster while talking. "We can't quit now. Look how wet this ground is. There must be water here somewhere."

I watch her work for another few minutes and say, "Let's see what else is around here. You need a break. We'll come back later." As we walk away, I'm aware that Pam is reluctantly following. She will be so surprised when we come back. We walk about twenty yards when I catch sight of movement in the underbrush. We stop stone still and watch the suspect spot. The movement comes again.

We shift our position so we can see our mystery guest. Pam stays right beside me and finally whispers, "Can you see what it is? It sounds like a bear."

I smile at Pam's comment and think of how much sound comes from a small animal in the underbrush. We finally move to a spot where we have a full view of the moving animal. I grin from ear to ear, "There's lunch!"

Pam's eyes follow my pointing finger to a clearing under a bush. With a shout, almost sounding like a protest, Pam yells, "Terry! It's a toad! We can't eat that!"

I have a challenging time containing my laughter as I answer. "We most certainly can, and we will. Look how big he is. He's about the size of a small basketball. He must be a Colorado River Toad."

"How are we ever going to eat him? I don't think I can even touch him."

"Don't think about eating him yet. Just think about catching him. I'll sit on this big log, and you slowly sneak up by him. Hit him over the head with your digging stick. He'll never know what happened."

"Terry, you can't be serious. You think we're going to eat this toad."

"I know we are. Most survival food doesn't come so easily. We're not going to let him slip away. Now get after him before he figures out what we're talking about."

Pam makes her way through the bushes complaining, "I can't believe I'm doing this." As she gets near the spot, the toad takes a giant leap into an open clearing.

"Hurry, Pam. He's out in the open, and you can get a good swing at him." Pam charges through the brush and into the clearing with her stick raised. She swings hard and misses hitting the ground.

"How could you miss him? You're only two feet away."

Looking a little embarrassed, Pam says, "I closed my eyes."

All I can get out is, "You what" before I break into uncontrollable laughter which Pam joins instantly. We both laugh until tears are running down our faces, and Pam just sits down on the ground.

When I finally catch my breath and can talk, I yell at Pam who is sitting in the clearing. "You can't do this to me. It takes away all my strength, and it makes my arm hurt. Are you sitting on that toad?"

With a start, Pam looks around. "No, he's just sitting here looking at me." With most of her laughter under control, she goes on. "Do I have to hit him?"

"I guess you don't, but the next entree won't be any easier. Most of the time you must work two days to get as much food as he has to offer. It's a good thing you don't have to catch and clean a live chicken when your mom sends you to the supermarket."

"I've never thought about it like that. I'll try again." This time Pam picks up her weapon and half looks as she brings the stick down hard on the toad's head. "Now, what do I do with him?"

"Pick him up and bring him along."

Pam stands studying the situation. Finally, she takes off her long-sleeved shirt and spreads it on the ground by the toad. She rolls him onto it with her stick and starts to tie up the corners to make a bag. She hears a movement behind her and turns quickly.

I see the maker of the new noise at the same time. "This is better than I could ever have hoped. It looks like his big brother. Pam, do your stuff again."

Before my words are out, Pam has knocked the second toad on the head and has him stuffed in the shirt. She says, "There should be plenty of food here now. I can hardly lift this little package. We better get back and check that fire. I sure don't want to light it from scratch again."

"Let's go back by way of your water hole."

Pam is the first to reach the excavation. She is totally surprised as she looks in the hole. "Terry, where did all of this water come from?"

As I join her, I can see that the hole is full of clear water. "It drains in from the sides when you give it a place to collect."

"Did you know it was going to do this?"

"I was sure hoping it would."

"Do I ever feel dumb! I bet you were having a good laugh watching me dig and asking if we couldn't stay just a little longer. You're getting back to your old self."

I can feel the total mood changing, and I try desperately to hold on to the rapport we have created. "I didn't mean to make you feel dumb. I'm deeply sorry. I just wanted to surprise you."

"Terry, I hate surprises. They take away any part I have in the decision-making process, and they cheat me out of learning. They are what my parents use on me to control everything in my life."

"Pam, I have never thought about it that way. I am so, so sorry. I will teach you the ins and outs of every survival skill we use—I promise I will be completely open and honest with you in all our communications, and absolutely no surprises of any kind. Both of our lives depend on it."

Pam looks at me with a hard glare and a set jaw. Finally, she nods her head and changes the subject, "Is this water good to drink, or do we have to put hot rocks in it?"

I welcome the shift with all my heart. "It will be the most heavenly water you have ever tasted. Have at it." I sit down on the rock again. Even though we have only been out for an hour, I am beginning to feel the deep fatigue again.

Pam drinks and hands a full bottle to me. "I think that's the best-tasting water I have ever had in my whole life. I could drink another quart."

I drink my full bottle and hand it back to Pam. "Drink as much as you can get inside. When you're in survival mode, it's best to store water in your body before you put it in your canteen. We shouldn't have any more water problems from here on out. That hole will fill up as fast as you empty it. It's just kind of a long walk from here to the cave. Do you recognize those green plants growing in the damp sand over there?"

Pam walks over and picks a stalk of the green leafy plant I am pointing to. "It's Miner's Lettuce, isn't it?"

"I'm impressed. You remember your plants. That's our salad for lunch. Pick a bunch, and you can wash it before we go back to the cave."

On the way back to the cave, Pam pumps me for information. "You look pretty wasted. You had better tell me how to fix our biology specimens on the way back. You need to crash when we get there, while I play cook."

I know Pam's right. All I can think about is lying down and going to sleep. My arm is even starting to ache a little. I hope my cooking directions will be clear enough to follow. Talking might also help me think of something else besides exhaustion. "The lettuce is easy. We just eat it. Split the toads up the middle of their bellies with the knife and take out their insides. You also need to skin them. Be careful with the two little glands on the top of their heads. They give off a liquid that stinks, but it won't hurt you. Once they're cleaned, put them on a stick, and roast until done."

We are to the cave when I glance up at the cactus on the sloping side of the canyon. "There's dessert if you manage it right. See those big, red, pear-shaped things at the end of the cactus sections. That's their fruit, and it looks ripe. If it is, it's delicious. The biggest trick is to pick it and singe it in the fire without getting filled with stickers. That's Prickly Pear, and it's covered with tiny cactus spines."

All conversation ends when we reach the cave. I collapse on my bed spot beside the fire and that's all I know until I hear, "Terry, Terry wake up. It's time for breakfast, lunch, and every other meal we've missed in the last two days."

I can hardly make myself come alive. Pam's voice seems so far away, and I want to stay asleep more than anything. She won't let me drift out again. "I know your body is tired, but you need some food to build more strength. Come alive long enough to eat, and then you can go back to dreamland."

I finally open my eyes, but my first sense to wake fully is my nose. I manage to speak as I roll over to look at the fire. "It smells like Thanksgiving dinner. Does that ever look good!"

My mind takes in the whole scene, and I am amazed at what I see. The toads have been cleaned, and both are threaded on two long green sticks. The sticks are long enough to reach across the fire and are supported at each end with forked sticks pushed into the ground. The barbecued meat is golden brown and dripping juice into the hotbed of roasting coals. On several single sticks being propped over the rocks which ring the fire are large purple-red Prickly Pears also dripping juice.

"My stomach is wide awake. You've been busy. After not being able to hit that poor little animal over the head, you've made remarkable progress."

"We almost didn't have the main course. It took everything I had to clean them. I just had to make myself think of other things, like how we were going to get out of here. After they were cleaned and skinned, then it was more like fixing chicken. I hope I can make my mind think it's eating chicken."

"If you got this far, your stomach will take over once you start eating. How did you get the Prickly Pears?"

"I wasn't excited about having a handful of cactus spines, so I went back to the spring and cut roasting willows. I made sure the sticks had little forks on the ends. I poked each pear with a stick and then cut it off the cactus. I lost a few, but I got back here with enough for dessert, I think. Anyway, there are lots more on the hill if you're still hungry. Enough of this talk, we need to eat it before it gets too done."

Pam takes the toads off the fire, cuts the sticks in half, and hands me two sticks with a skewered toad on the end. "Sorry I didn't get out the best china and silver for this grand occasion. We'll just have to eat off the cooking sticks. Can you manage that with one hand?"

"As long as I have the sticks to hang on to, it's probably easier than if I had to use the silver."

I raise my golden-brown treasure to my mouth and take a bite. "I don't think you'll even have to pretend. It tastes like the best chicken I ever had. It could do with a little salt, but that's hardly noticeable. You're a great cook."

I can tell Pam is still having trouble with her mindset. She is just staring at her dinner. "Pam, don't think about it. Talk to me about something else, and just eat. Tell me what you're going to do after you graduate next year. Are you going to college?"

Pam looks at me. "Are you sure it's good? It smells delicious, and I'm so hungry. I just can't forget it's an ugly, warty toad."

"Try talking to me about anything, and just take a bite. I see you've been busy. It looks like you've collected enough firewood to last for a week." All the while I am talking, I'm eating. If I can just get Pam to take the first bite, I know she couldn't stop either.

"My stomach says it's going to be sick if I don't eat, and my mind says it's going to be sick if I do. My stomach is winning."

I smile as I watch Pam close her eyes and take a little taste. She holds it in her mouth for a long while and then swallows. "Terry, your right, this does taste a little like chicken. I think I can do this."

We both fall into silent eating. Many thoughts run through my mind as we feast. I think of how fortunate we are to have a survival meal where we might get full and even have a little leftover. This is unheard of when one is trying to eat off the land. I also decide it is not so bad that Pam and I ended up together. Mrs. Scott was right. At least we can take care of each other. Pam is doing a super job. She pulls me out of my silent world when she asks "Did you get full? There are still a couple of piping-hot prickly pears minus the prickles. I even have some toad left if you want some more."

"I'm stuffed. I didn't finish my toad either. Let's wrap them in leaves, put them in the back of the cave, and save them for a late supper. You won't have to look for any more food today."

"That sounds wonderful to me—Terry I keep wondering, with your busy life when did you learn to mountain climb?"

"I started when I was about six years old. My brothers all wanted to climb, so it became part of our annual survival trip each summer. Dad had climbed some when he was a teenager. He got books, and we all studied and practiced on Saturdays. Climbing gear became a staple part of our backpacking equipment. By the time I was sixteen, I could always get up places my brothers wouldn't even attempt because of my size, weight, and strength ratio."

Pam nods her head in understanding and asks, "Terry, do you know what I want now? A nice long nap."

"I'll bet you're tired after staying up most of the night and working all morning. Unbelievably, I could go back to sleep again. Let's find a soft rock in the sun."

We don't have to go far to find the perfect spot. We also don't have to wait long until we were both sound asleep.

CHAPTER 11

I jerk awake with a start which sends a bolt of pain through my arm. Why am I so suddenly awake? Something has brought me from dreamland, but what? I'm then hit on the arm and head at the same time with raindrops. I breathe a little sigh of relief. At least it isn't anything major. I roll over on my side and shake Pam's leg, "Pam, Pam, wake up. I think you'd sleep right through this storm if I'd let you. Let's get back to the cave. You don't want to start another night, wet."

Pam sleepily groans, "What's a little rain. My body feels like it could sleep forever. Come back for me tomorrow."

"Okay. You and George enjoy the night."

Turning over and fully awake Pam asks, "Who's, George?"

"I thought it was the name of your pet cougar. I am sure he'd love to cuddle up with you out here tonight."

"All right, you win." Pam jumps to her feet continuing, "I almost forgot about the fire. We've been asleep out here for a long time. I can see the sun sinking behind those thunderheads. I sure hope the fire hasn't gone out."

With Pam holding on to me, we both head back to the cave. We reach the entrance just as the rain starts pouring. I watch as Pam stirs the fire around with a stick searching for live coals, "Pam, you've done such a thorough job on that fire it'll take three days for it to burn out when we leave. You've got at least a two-inch bed of coals."

"It's a good thing. Getting this fire started was such a miracle, I'm not sure I'd ever be able to do it again. The thought of it going out keeps my stomach churned up. I think we do need a little more wood for the night. If the rain lets up before it's completely dark, we better get some more water and another load of logs."

I am looking out of the cave's entrance at the sky. "I don't think we're going to get much water out of this cloud. It started off dumping, but it's letting up fast. We could almost go now. Before we head out again could you take two or three of those willow branches you used for roasting sticks and peel off the bark?"

Pam looks at me questioningly, "What trick do you have up your sleeve now?'

I explain, "We only have six of your pain pills left, and I don't know if I can sleep without them. The bark of the willow is supposed to have the same chemicals found in aspirin. If I chew on some bark it might help with the pain enough, we can save your pills for tonight and maybe the next night."

Pam peels the bark and makes a small ball for me. As she hands it to me, she laughs, "I won't tell anybody you were chewing on our little adventure." I pull a face, stuff the wad in my mouth, and begin chomping. Pam finishes building up the fire and joins me at the door. "Let's go. That fine mist won't hurt anything unless you'd sooner stay here and rest some more."

"Believe it or not, I think I'm finally about rested out."

"Good, let's go. I think we have about two hours of light. We might even have time to pull off some more bark for pillows."

"Pam, I'm sure glad you say 'we' even when I just tag along, and you do all the work."

Pam is silent for a minute before she answers. "I don't particularly like being out here alone especially when it starting to get dark, and I'm sure George isn't far from home." She goes on with a lighter, joking tone. "Besides, you might find something else for us to eat."

We both laugh as we approach the spring. I sit down on my large rock while Pam drinks and then fills the bottle for me. As she turns around and focuses to hand me the water bottle, her expression changed instantly. Watching, I can see real terror in her eyes, and I freeze every muscle. The only things moving are my thoughts. It must be a snake, and it must be right beside me. I want to shout, Pam! Please don't stop using your head. And please do something quickly. Instead, I maintain my stone position.

Pam finally whispers, "Terry, don't move. There's a huge snake beside you."

Pam looks around and sees a dead limb behind her. The pole is about six feet long and two inches in diameter. She moves slowly back away from me and the snake toward the weapon. When she bends down to pick up the stick, the grass rustles, and the snake begins to shake its tail sounding the rattle alarm.

My thoughts rush on. This rattlesnake must be able to hear my heart pounding. It's so loud it feels like my head is going to burst. I hope I don't faint. Heavenly Father! We need your help again. Please don't abandon us now after saving us from the flash flood. Please bless Pam to know what to do. Go easy Pam, but please hurry. From the sound of those rattles, he must be fifty feet long. Despite all the visions of horror dancing in my head, I'm still a lifeless statue.

Pam moves toward the snake with the outstretched stick. She keeps it at the snake's eye level and moves the end back and forth just a little as she creeps closer. The snake began to move with the movement of the pole and tenses for the fight. When she gets the end of the stick about eight inches from the snake, she pokes hard at him. The snake lunges off the rock to strike at the stick.

The instant he is on the ground, Pam forces the end of her pole under him and lifts it at the same time. In a sideward flip, she sends the snake into the air. He is almost five feet long and so heavy Pam only moves him about ten feet. When he lands, Pam is right there with a basketball-sized rock lifted above her head. She brings it down quickly on the snake with a smashing force, which buries its head in the dirt. Its body thrashes and twitches, but its head is stuck under the rock. We both just stare at the undulating snake. I finally whisper, "That was a perfect tennis smash if I ever saw one."

Pam moves to me, "Are you all, right? He didn't bite you, did he?"

I look at Pam and realize I am still not speaking aloud. I swallow hard and try to get out words. "I'm okay, at least my body's okay. I don't know about my heart. I thought it was going to explode." I take a deep breath and go on a little slower. "I've never felt so helpless in my entire life. I owe you a big one."

Pam speaks as she turns and heads back to the spring. "I think it's time we stopped counting. We better get moving. We don't have much light left."

I call out, "What about the snake?"

Pam turns and looks at me incredulously, "You're not thinking of eating that hideous thing, are you?"

"I told you survival food is hard to come by. We can't let it go to waste. Besides, it tastes better than a toad."

Pam finally hangs her head in resignation, "Okay, what do I do?"

"Cut off his head where his body is coming out from under the rock. Open his belly cavity with the knife and scrape out the innards. The cavity isn't long; most of him is good meat. When we get back to the cave, you can either skin him and roast him over the coals or leave the skin on for now and cook him in a pit like we did the chickens at camp."

Pam swallows hard, "I will clean him here so I can get cleaned up where we have water. We don't have any foil to cook him in a pit."

I'm glad Pam's going to try cooking this snake. I explain, "Dig the pit and build a fire in the bottom just like for chicken. Once you have a bed of coals, put in a layer of big leaves, and lay the snake on top of it. Cover it with more leaves and then build more fire on top just like you have always done. Once there are coals on top, cover them with dirt and let the fire do its thing. Oh, before you cook him, cut off the rattles and keep them for your trophy cabinet."

When the snake is ready and wrapped in a bundle of leaves, Pam turns to me. "Do you think you can walk on your own back to the cave while I carry your rattling treasure and gather some more wood and bark?"

I slowly stand, taking a few slow steps I say, "I think I can if I have a walking stick." Pam hands me the weapon she hurled the snake with. I nod my head to say yes.

Pam hands me the bottle for a drink, fills it again, and hands it back to me. "Can you take this water also?"

We walk back slowly, Pam gathering wood as we go. She drops her armful on the woodpile and hurries back out for more. I move to my sitting spot beside the fire and put on a couple of large pieces of wood. Pam is back in minutes with another load. She throws it on the pile and rushed back out.

On the way she says, "If I hurry, I can make one more trip." She slips out into the almost dark of night. She is gone a little longer this time. When she returns, she has a huge arm full of juniper bark. She quickly sets her juniper pile on the ground and steps just outside the cave entrance to a pile of boulders. There is enough light from the fire to start making a cooking pit. She uses my walking stick to pry up rocks and toss them aside. Gradually the rocks gave way to a sandy floor. Digging is easy then. Before long she has a fire made, the snake bundle on the coals, more coals on top, and finally a covering of sand on the pit.

She comes back into the cave and seats herself by the fire drawing her juniper bark close by, "It's pillow time again. I sure hope we'll get to use them all night tonight."

I realize we are in for the night. I also realize, for the first time since we started our cave-dwelling experience, I don't have much pain. The willow bark is working wonderfully. I am pondering if this natural remedy would help through the night when Pam breaks the silence. "This survival stuff is awesome, but I have one big frustration with it. My long hair is always in the way, and I can't figure out anything to tie it in place. My hair things are in my pack."

I think for a quick second, "Pam, bring some of that juniper bark you're making into pillows and come and sit right here beside me," pointing to the ground on my left side. "This is a two-handed skill, but if you will be my left hand, I'll show you how to make a tie for your hair." Pam quickly sits beside me. I take the long juniper fibers with my right hand and lay out two small bundles on my stretched-out leg. I pinch the two bundles together at one end, "Bring your left hand over in front of me and hold these ends tight between your thumb and first finger." I show her how to twist and turn the fibers to make a cord.

Pam watches carefully as I twist about an inch of the fibers into a cord. She breaks into a smile, "I get it. Let me try with both hands." I transfer my work into Pam's right hand. She twists and turns slowly at first and then began to fall into a rhythm. Looking troubled she asks, "What if I want it longer? I am running out of fibers."

I pick up some more fibers, "Keep your left-hand pinching and lay these fibers on top of one bundle and twist them in as you go. It is best to stagger the places where you add to each bundle, so you don't create a weak spot. When the cord is as long as you want it, tie an overhand knot, and then tie a knot at the top where you started. If you need it stronger then you simply twist two cords together. I can't believe how fast you learn. Your twine looks like you have been doing this all your life."

Pam is fascinated with her new skill. When the cord is about ten inches long, she ties the knots, moves back to her pile of juniper fibers, and starts another cord. After working in silent consecration for a while she says, "Terry, why do you hate me?"

Oh no! I say to myself. This is not where I want to go tonight. I quickly answer and try to head the conversation in another direction. "I don't hate you. How could I? You just saved my life, again."

"I don't mean particularly hate. And maybe hate isn't the right word. Why do you dislike me more than anyone else you know or have ever known in your whole life? Remember, you promised to have complete, open, and honest, communication with me."

"I guess I set myself up for this didn't I?"

"You did, and I promise to be just as open and honest with you. Now talk to me, Terry Masters."

"Okay," I meet and hold Pam's eyes, seriously replying, "It isn't even so much I dislike you. I just want you and everyone else to know I'm as good as you."

"Terry, I, and everyone else know you are as good if not better than me. We each have some strong points, but we are pretty much equal. What are you talking about?"

"Look, Pam. You have everything. You have a mom and dad who watch out for you. You have money coming out of your ears. You play tennis at the country club and get private lessons every day. You've got your very own car, and you have a wardrobe of all the latest styles which never quits. I don't have any of those things, but I still think I'm as good as you are."

Pam moans aloud and stares at the fire. "Oh Terry, appearances are not what they seem. I'd trade any one of those things if I could be what you are."

Now it is my turn to be taken back. In a questioning tone, I ask, "What do you mean?" with emphasis on the "you."

"Just what I said, I'd trade any one of the things on the list you just rattled off to have what you have. You've got brains. You're cute. You're talented. You're skilled. You're independent. You make your own decisions, and you're the best tennis player I've ever played against."

Anger starts welling in me as I fire back. "You beat me, didn't you?"

"No... I didn't beat you. My dad, Mr. D. Fletcher, did. You are a much better player than I am. At least you were on the State finals day. You don't know how I've kicked myself repeatedly for not following my feelings. I should have walked off the court when he yelled at you. I was so embarrassed, but I didn't have the guts to face his wrath. I have made up my mind it'll never happen again."

I flip out a comment I almost wish I hadn't made before my sentence is through. "You mean he's not your ace in the hole when things get rough?"

Pam is now trying to control a little anger. "I guess it looks that way from the outside. Just because you've got a parent there with you, it doesn't mean he's there to support you. My dad's in it for himself. If I win, somehow, he thinks it makes him look good. If I lose, he thinks he looks bad. It took a long time for me to figure him and the tennis out. I have played ever since I can remember. He's always been there pushing me to be better. Once I saw one of his old college yearbooks. He played on his college tennis team, but he was always the last man listed. I understood where I fit in one day when I overheard him talking to one of his old college tennis buddies. He said that I was becoming the tennis player he always knew he could be. I think what he's doing is trying to live his sports life over through me. He also has never let me play doubles. That way he won't have to share the spotlight with anyone when he wins."

My anger is gone; I can't believe what I'm hearing. "If it bothers you, why haven't you talked to him about it?"

"I tried. Once I told him how embarrassed I was. I even said I didn't want to play anymore if he was going to make digging comments on the side."

"What did he say?"

"He took me on an old-fashioned guilt trip. He yelled about how thankful I should be for all the time and money he has invested for me to learn how to play. He said he only wanted me to get what was rightfully mine. Then he said if I didn't want him around, he wouldn't come. My mother then jumped all over me about being rude and ungrateful to my father."

"Is he like that at every match?"

"Oh no, if I'm winning, he's quite polite. He even claps and complements the opposition if he's sure I'm going to win. He is my motivation for trying harder to win. He doesn't have to make degrading remarks from the sideline. I've never seen him congratulate anyone who's beaten me."

"How was he at the Invitation Tournament the week before camp? How did you do anyway? I never heard."

"I didn't go."

My mouth drops open in surprise, "You didn't go? What do you mean you didn't go? After beating me, you were seeded number one in that tournament. How could you not go?"

Pam answers slowly with tears in her eyes. "When you play in the amateur tournaments, there's all kinds of illegal underhanded play going on. When my dad would intimidate my opponent, he would always say he was just helping me get what I rightly deserved. After his remarks in our match, I realized he would do anything to not lose including destroying my integrity. After our match, I told my Dad I would never play tennis again. I have not picked up my racket since that awful day. Terry, you have no idea how bad I felt about that match. I just didn't know how to talk to you about it. You have a right to hate me. We did steal your State Title."

"Pam, you can't just quit. You're too good of a player. You like to play, don't you?"

"Even though my dad started me to fulfill his dreams, I do like to play. I'm at a point, though, if I can't beat someone with my skills and my brains, I'd sooner lose. Even more, I'd sooner not play if someone else has to play dirty from the side to help me win."

"Pam, I'm sorry. I just figured if your parents were there, they were there helping you. It sounds like I get more moral support on the court from my brother than you do from your dad. What about your mom?"

"She's much the same; her area of pride is simply different. You know the unlimited clothes supply you mentioned, I hate it. Since my mom is the buying agent for the Teen Fashion Shop, she figures I should be the best-dressed girl in the state."

I laugh, "Doesn't sound like something I'd hate."

"You would before long. Terry, I have never gone to the store by myself and picked out one outfit of clothes. She orders what she thinks I'll look good in. She even tries to tell me which outfit I'll wear each day. If I'm feeling independent, I'll argue. If I don't want a hassle, I just let her decide."

I try to lighten the conversation a little. "I guess I do get to choose which T-shirt I'll wear with my jeans."

With determination in her voice, Pam goes on. "Terry, your clothes don't make you what you are. Because you wear much the same thing all the time, people look past the outer layer to get to know the real you. Do people ever talk to you about what you're wearing? I doubt it. They talk to you about what you're doing, and about what you feel and think. You can be real."

I am a little perplexed, "What do people talk to you about?"

"Clothes! What else. They think fashion dressing is all my mind is capable of. I can't even get ready for a tennis match without someone asking which coordinated outfit I'm going to wear. I hate the image. I just want people to know the real me living in the clothes."

"Why don't you just wear something dull and plain?"

Pam shakes her head, "Sounds easy, doesn't it? Well, I tried. I snuck out and bought myself a pair of jeans and a T-shirt. I knew I'd never get out the front door with them on, so I had Carol take them to school with her. I changed in the locker room before school started.

"It just happened my mom ran into the principal at a Rotary Club meeting that morning, and he made comments about my new image. My mom came to school, pulled me out of class, and created a horrible scene in the hall. She made me change into a hideous outfit she had brought. I couldn't look anyone in the eye for a week. At least you get to choose what you wear."

I laugh a little, "Some choice. I can wear jeans and T-shirts, or T-shirts and jeans. I did manage to talk my brother into a couple of blouses this year. I probably worry as much about what people are thinking about my clothes as you do. The only difference is they never say a word to me about my marvelous wardrobe. They just talk to each other behind my back about how I dress like a tramp. It would be fun to have just a couple of your clothes problems."

"Terry, the outfit you had on at the dance was fantastic. Everyone was commenting about how great you looked."

"I'll bet they were saying, 'It's about time she wore something decent.' That's the first real dressy outfit I've had since I outgrew the clothes I had when my parents died."

"Won't your brothers let you buy some dresses? Don't they know you're a girl, and girls need those kinds of things?"

My mind flashes back to the night Tom gave me the new outfit for the dance. He had been excited and yet sad when I modeled the new clothes.

His words still ring in my mind. "I wish I could give you more."

I then answer Pam. "Won't, isn't the problem. There just isn't any money right now. I don't know how long Tom had to save or how many extra hours he had to work to buy me that outfit."

I am silent for a moment and decide to tell Pam more. "When my parents were killed and our family situation finally settled down, the four of us held a counsel about our future and the insurance. I am sure glad I have three older brothers who have their priorities in order. They set up a plan for the insurance money so the house and living expenses would be taken care of, and each brother would have money for his college education and mission. Each brother agreed if their schooling were paid for, they would work while going to school to pay their living expenses and would try hard for a scholarship. I was already doing well on the piano and my parents had just bought a baby Grand Piano before they left us. It was decided I would not work while going to school but put my extra time into practicing the piano. There is money for me each month, but it mostly goes for piano music and tennis clothes, shoes, and rackets. I also have a couple of skirts that I wear to church with my blouses."

I go silent, a little embarrassed by my disclosure. Pam looks at me as if deciding. She seems hesitant as she says, "I just always figured you didn't like dresses, or you worried about more important things than being in the fashion race. Would you wear some if you had them?"

I look at Pam and smile a little, "It would sure be fun to have a choice."

"Maybe I can help. My closet is only so big. When new clothes come in every week, old clothes must go out. Mom is strange in that way. She puts all this time and money into the getting, but she couldn't care less what I do with the ones going out. She doesn't even care which ones I get rid of. I give them away to girls at school. I wear them so little no one knows they used to be mine. The world just thinks the girls bought new outfits. I never say anything and neither do they. Terry, would you take some outfits if I gave them to you?"

I'm stunned. Is this the same girl I have tried to best at every turn in my life? This person I've competed with since I could remember; is she offering to help? I have little reason to doubt Pam's sincerity after the last two days. I want to say yes, but the emotions flooding inside will not let me say anything.

Pam senses my struggle and carries on the conversation. "I know it would be hard when you've worked to be on top by yourself. No one would ever know but you and me. You don't have to decide right now, just think about it."

Pam changed the subject, "Do you like Paul?"

I lift my head and stare at Pam. I want to say, 'What is this? Open every feeling I have night?' Instead, I try taking the offense, "I thought you were going with Paul." This is my chance to check out her feelings for him.

Pam laughs, "You don't know very much about me, do you? Paul and I have grown up together. Our parents do everything together, so we've spent lots of time together. He's like the best brother a girl could have. We talk about everything, and he takes care of me when I need help. The only people who think we're going together are our parents. They think they've created this ideal match. Paul and I think they've created an ideal brother and sister. We let them think what they want, and we do what we want. Right now, I'm kind of going with Rick."

I am cautious with the little excitement growing inside, but I stay on the attack. "What about the dance? Weren't you with Paul?"

Pam thinks for a second, "I guess that's what it looked like. Paul's been taking a mechanics class and playing master mechanic on my car. It died in the street out in front of the school the night of the dance. I had to get him to see if he could unfix whatever he had fixed in the morning. It didn't take long. He came back to the dance to find you, but you had gone. Boy, did he give me a bad time. He would like to go out with you. He just doesn't know if it would bother you to be seen with a boy who's dumber in math than you are. You just say the word, and you'll have a date, although it might have to be right after camp. He is leaving on his mission in September."

Since I promised to be open and honest, I decide to share my feelings. "Pam, I like him a lot. We got to know each other well in our math tutoring sessions. The more I got to know him, the more I liked him. He's smart, quick-witted, caring, and on top of that devilishly handsome. He did finally ask me out on a date the week before camp."

Before I can change the subject, she asks, "Where did he take you?"

Again, I decide to be honest, "We went on a hike up the trail to the hot spring."

"Paul took you to the hot springs?" she says in total shock.

"We passed by the hot pots; it wasn't our destination. We went to the end of the trail high up on the mountainside. The view up there is breathtaking, and there's a small brook with a fire pit beside it to cook steaks. When we passed the hot springs, Jerk Jake was skinny dipping with his friends. He tried to get us to join them, but all Paul could do was turn red. We made a hasty parting to continue our hike."

"Jake is such a loser. He's tried every trick possible to get me alone with him, but I know what he wants. I refuse to trash my temple recommend. If I've made it through my tennis tournaments staying clean, I know how to side-step that slimeball—How was your date anyway?"

We've hit the line as to how much I'll share; I remember my advice to Paul, I smile, "It was the most romantically beautiful day I have ever spent."

Now Pam is almost panicked, "Terry, you didn't, did you? Paul must go on his mission, but he likes you an awful lot."

"No worries, Pam. Paul is husband material, but both of us are way too young to get married. He is still going on his mission, and we both came back out of the canyon temple worthy."

Taking advantage of her stunned silence, "My stomach thinks it's time for a look in your fire pit, how about yours?"

Pam glances at the fire pit and seems to be thinking, I don't know if I'm hungry or not. She slowly gets up and begins uncovering our serpent dinner which is cooking in the pit. She scrapes everything aside and finally comes to the bundle of the snake. She picks it up with the fire tongs and a stick and places the rattler by me. Then her face lights up. "I think I will finish my toad and have prickly pears. I'll try the snake in the morning." She goes to the back of the cave to retrieve her toad package and cactus pears.

Picking up a bark bundle from the rock shelf in the rear of the cave, she brings it to the fire. She starts opening her toad package, and I open the leaf package to the cooked snake. I look up, "Pam can I take my knife for a second? I need to split the skin." Pam hands me the knife and begins pinching off a piece of her cold toad. I split the skin and then drop the knife screaming. I grimace as a wave of pain stabs me.

Pam is instantly at my side, "Terry, what's happening?

"I think all my pain meds have worn off. I don't feel so good."

"Oh no, we let the medicine level in your blood get too low. You need to take two more of the pain pills and drink the whole water bottle." Pam also asks, "Have you used our outhouse just outside the cave entrance."

Lying back against the cave wall and trying not to move at all, I reply, "Not since morning, but I don't need to go. I just want to lay down and sleep."

Shaking her head, Pam says, "I was afraid of that. I've also let you get more dehydrated. I have your pillow finished right here." She hands the shredded juniper bark ball to me as she moves to get the full water bottle and two more pain pills.

I take the pills, drink all the water, and am positioning my pillow when I look at Pam and think of how I'm trusting and counting on her help. The words are hard, but I try to tell her how I feel. "Pam, I'm sure glad you know as much about treating injuries as you do. I wasn't so sure when you were working on Alison, but I don't know how I'll ever be able to thank you for everything you're doing for me. I'm sorry I've been such an absolute slob.

Pam lowers her head and her voice as she speaks, "I probably got a little carried away with Alison. You do everything so much better than I do at camp. I just couldn't resist the chance to show off and put you down a little."

I think of all the put-downs I have handed Pam, those planned, and those that just happen. "Don't worry about that. I more than had it coming. I'm glad you're here, and you know what you know. I have a long awkward pause as I look at her. "Pam, do you pray?"

It is such a quick change; it catches her completely off guard with nothing to say. After a long moment, a very few well-chosen words come out, "Do you mean pray or PRAY?"

"I mean really PRAY, really talk to a God who listens and answers prayers."

"I think the first time I have ever really prayed is when we were running back down this little canyon in the rain yesterday. The second time was when you were trying to get me up over the ledge and the wall of water hit. I kept praying and crying the whole time we were sliding. When we stopped and the water kept pushing, it felt like we were both being held on to. I tried it again when I couldn't get the fire started and again an answer came. I was praying the whole time I was fighting your snake and following the impressions that came into my mind."

I cut her off before she can go on, "The night my mom and dad were killed, we had had a family prayer before they left. I even remember Rick blessing them to come home safe. When they didn't come home, I decided God doesn't answer prayers if he was there at all. We kept having family prayers and blessings on the food, but I never really prayed by myself again, until yesterday in the flood. The Lord was there, and He has watched out for us; I've been such a fool."

"Terry, you're not the only fool. I've said a lot of words in prayers, but I don't think I have ever really prayed from my heart with real intent until yesterday. My family has so much, we have no real needs, so prayers are just words. I can see now I don't have to be alone in my struggles to find my independence. I just need to pray with the same energy I have these last two days."

I can tell the pills are starting to work as my thought process and answers are slowing down. "Pam, before those pain pills take me over completely, can we have a prayer together? Someone needs a little help finding us."

I fall asleep thinking about how good it feels to have two new friends,

Pam, and my Heavenly Father.

CHAPTER 12

When I wake the next morning, I can feel the warmth of the bright fire. As all my senses begin to function, I realize the sunrise is long past. I look around without getting up and see prickly pears warming on the fire, a full bottle of water beside me, and Pam is nowhere in sight. I think to myself; I must still be out of it. Pam's fed the fire all night, built it up this morning, has been to the spring for water, has breakfast ready, and I didn't hear a thing. This feels a little disconcerting as I am used to being aware of movements around me both day and night. I have a reputation at camp that no one can sneak up on me asleep or awake. Now, they could drag me away by my toes, and I would be oblivious.

While I am contemplating my consciousness level, Pam walks in with a huge armload of wood. "Good morning, Terry. Welcome to the daytime. I'm glad you're awake; I was going to tickle you if you weren't. It's a beautiful day. It rained last night, and the water level is about chest-high, but the sun is shining on the mountains and the clouds are gone. The water level could be down this afternoon or evening.

I watch as Pam drops her load of wood, and then I do a double take. "Good morning, Pocahontas. You look like you belong right in the middle of this survival scene."

Pam blushes a little, "I thought if we are doing all of this living off the land stuff, I might look well my part. When I started to fix my hair with the string we made last night, it came to me that braids might work best. They keep my hair out of the way, they don't get everything tangled in them, and they keep my hair clean. It took forever to get the snarls and junk out of my hair this morning. The Native Americans did know what they were doing.

Pam's expression turns to one of excitement, and her eyes sparkle as she says, "Terry, I have something to show you." She rushes out of the cave and returns instantly holding a carrot-looking plant in one hand and a giant mushroom in the other. "I found these, and I want to know if we can eat them.

I reach for the ferny-looking plant with the white carrot and ask, "Where did you find this?"

"It was growing in the soggy ground back by the cattails. It looked like a carrot top, so I pulled it up to see what it had on the bottom. It's like a carrot, only it's white."

I tell her it's water hemlock and ask, "Do you remember Socrates?"

Pam questioningly answers, "Isn't he the philosopher from Athens who was accused of leading the city's youth astray with his philosophy and put to death?"

"Wow, you have a sharp memory. Do you remember how he was executed?"

"I think he drank some poisonous something."

"Pam you are so smart. Now we'll just enlarge your knowledge base. He was given a cup of hemlock tea by the executioner which he drank."

Pam's excitement fades quickly as she bursts out, "Terry, I am so sorry. I could have killed us both. I won't pick any more stuff unless you are there. I want so badly to have the knowledge you have, but I don't have a clue how to get it. This toadstool is probably poisonous too. I have never seen one this big."

"Pam if you have a burning desire to learn about all the edible things in the out-of-doors, I'll teach you all I can and open the ways for you to teach yourself. The worst thing you could do is stop asking questions. Here's the rule, check out every possibility, but eat nothing until you know it's safe. We wouldn't have died because I know it's poison. If I didn't know, we wouldn't eat it this time, but we would research it to know for the next time."

"Now, let me look at your mushroom." Pam hands me the ten-inch diameter plant she is holding. "This, Pamula Fletcher, is on the other end of the eating spectrum. Wars have been fought over this piece of goodness in Japan. This is a Cep from the Boleti family of edible fungi. Come closer so you can look at it."

I turn it over so she can see the underneath of the mushroom and point out it has a spongy surface and not gills. I tell her, "All of the mushrooms with this spongy bottom are edible except the bright red ones. They're not poisonous, but too spicey hot to eat. This one will be the treat of our trip. Cut it into half-inch slices and lay them on the coals. We'll turn them in five minutes and then enjoy a real gourmet treat."

"Terry, will you teach me? I feel so bad when I can't give our campers more knowledge about the wilds we visit—sorry, I got carried away. I haven't even asked you how you are doing this morning. How are you?"

I laugh a little, "When we get home, we'll go up our canyons, and I'll teach you a whole new kind of meal preparation. I even have books back at Lightning Mountain to get you started."

"I feel much better than last night, but I am growing weaker. I don't think I can even get to our outhouse without you holding on to me."

Pam looks closely at me and sighs, "we pushed you too hard yesterday. I brought you some more willows to chew on, and I'll get you another bottle of water as soon as you finish this one. I think you had better stay close to our mansion today." After helping me to the outhouse and back into the cave, Pam heads to the spring for more water and more wood. When she returns, I heard her drop the wood outside before coming into the cave.

When she enters the cave, I questioningly ask, "Are you making another fire outside?"

Pam smiles, "I've been thinking and praying hard this morning while you sawed logs. It came to me that the canyon floor or stream could be full of people looking for us, but we wouldn't hear them, and they would never guess this little paradise exists. Left on their own, rescuers would never find us. I thought I would go native all the way and make a signal fire, or at least a smoky fire. Anyone on the canyon floor would see the smoke or even a plane flying overhead if I built it on our infamous shelf. First though, I'm hungry, and I have a confession to make. I ate the leftovers of both toads last night. So, I guess it's snake or snake for breakfast."

I laugh, "The smoky fire is a brilliant idea, and I prefer a snake for breakfast along with your mushroom." Pam goes back to our food shelf and grabs the snake bundled in leaves. She sits next to me and unwraps our meal. I pull back the split skin and pinch off a piece of white snake meat. As I am placing it in my mouth, I notice Pam's look of hesitation again.

"Come on Pam. Quit thinking about it. Just pinch off a piece and put it in your mouth. It's much better than toad even if it still needs a little salt." Pam pinches off a little meat, closes her eyes, and puts it in her mouth. It's only been in her mouth an instant when she opens her eyes and reaches eagerly for more.

Together we eat half of the rattler, all the mushroom, and three prickly pears each. Pam sighs with satisfaction and announces, "The mushroom was the best I have ever eaten, even better than in any five-star restaurant my dad takes us to. Now, I'll start the signal fire!" She heads out of the cave.

I stretch out and relax; my willow bark pain reliever is starting to work. I don't fall asleep, but instead, offer another prayer of thanksgiving for our situation and a plea to be rescued. As I finish my silent prayer, Pam rushes through the entrance and grabs the water bottle. She calls back as she runs out, "I am going to keep you hydrated today!"

I offer another prayer of gratitude for this new friend I'm making. In less than ten minutes Pam is back with the water. I'm still awed by her new survival image. Pam hands the bottle to me, "Drink up!"

I protest, "You first this time."

Pam waves her hand, "I drink a full bottle every time I go to the spring. This water is all for you, and it needs to be in your body, not sitting in the bottle on the ground." I take the bottle and drink all the water; I can't believe I am still extremely thirsty. Pam grabs the empty bottle and returns to the spring for a refill. When she returns, she lays the bottle beside me and sits down by the fire. "Terry, what are you going to do after you graduate next year?"

My countenance falls a little, "I'm going on to school, I think."

"What do you mean, 'I think?' Is there a doubt in your mind?"

I haven't consciously thought about it. As we talk, I realize I am building doubts. "For as far back as I can remember, I've been on my way to study music after I finished high school. My mom thought I'd be good enough to get into Juilliard School of Music."

"Terry, that's neat. Isn't that one of the top music schools in the country?"

"Some say it's the best. All I know is the only way I could ever afford to go there is to get a big scholarship. I'm supposed to have my scholarship recital in December. I'm not sure they take one-handed piano players." With a crack in my voice, I ask, "Do you think there's any way I'll be able to use my hand again?"

Pam's tone becomes one of cheerful encouragement as she senses my anxiety. "I think there are more chances you will than you won't." She continues as she moves to sit beside me. "This is probably as good a time as any to check that wound and redress it."

I slip the sling over my head, and Pam starts removing the bandage strips which are holding the dressing in place. She slowly lifts the pad covering the wound because it's sticking with dried blood; she nods with approval.

"This looks good. The sides of the cut are together and there's no sign of infection. You're a perfect patient."

I'm looking the other way, remembering how gross the cut had looked when I saw it the first time. "I don't think I can look at it. It makes me sick just thinking about what it looked like."

"It does look good. You just need a new dressing on it. Oh, for the want of a good first aid kit. I guess a piece of the sleeve from my shirt will have to do. Terry, you're not going to pass out on me, are you?"

With my eyes closed and my head turned away, I answer, "I'm okay.

Just hurry and get it fixed back up. It feels a lot better when it's bandaged."

When Pam has all the bandage strips tied back together and sling in place, she takes hold of my clenched hand and gently straightens one of my fingers. She takes a little pointed stick and pokes my finger again. "Can you feel that in your finger?"

I am still leaning back against the wall with my eyes squeezed shut. "It still feels like you're trying to make my finger into a pincushion."

"This is excellent, Terry. You still have feeling in your fingers. That's a plus for your nerve." Pam goes on, "We desperately need to get you to a hospital ASAP." I begin to feel a ray of hope.

I turn the conversation trying to get my thoughts off my injured arm. "Pam, I think I can guess the kind of school you're going to, medical school."

"I wish it were that easy. The only reason I became a paramedic was to get out of the house. Dad wouldn't let me work, nor would he let me put time into music. Volunteering at the hospitals in the evenings was an acceptable activity he could brag about.

Pam hesitates, "After graduation? That's a good question. It would be easiest to go be a hermit. I'm going to conflict with my father again, and I'm not sure I'm up to the battle."

I look at her questioningly, "Why the conflict? Doesn't he want you to go to school?"

"It's not going to college, but it's the where and what. I told you I am filling my dad's dream to be a sensational tennis star. His dream hasn't ended. He told me I didn't need to fill out any college or scholarship applications; he would take care of it all."

I still do not understand, "With your tennis ranking, your grades, and your voice you could get a top scholarship to any school you choose in the whole United States."

"Want, Terry. That's the key, what I want. I don't want to be a tennis player for the rest of my life. I want to sing. I wouldn't mind playing on a college team, but I don't want to be a professional tennis player. I want to see how far I can go in the music world. I think I'd even like to teach music. My father is trying to get me into a school that turns out tennis players ready to turn professional."

I can finally feel her helplessness, "Pam, you have to live with yourself for the rest of your life. You can only become what you have the vision to see. If you can't picture yourself as a professional tennis player, you'll never be one, no matter how much your dad wants it. Why don't you toughen your skin and just take music in college."

Pam shakes her head with a little laugh. "At this point, my problem resembles yours, money. My dad said he would never throw away his money on sending me to school to major in music or teaching. He said it was a waste of fine talent, and he wasn't going to waste money too. He thinks if he won't give me any money, he can control me to be the tennis player he wants. If I go into music, I will need to support myself. I need a scholarship too."

"Have you applied to a school with a good vocal music program? You sing well enough. Why don't you just go for it?"

"I don't know exactly how to do that. My father's blocked me from being involved in the admissions process in any way."

"I've watched my three brothers fill out applications and earn enough scholarships to completely put themselves through school. After we're back home, come over to my house, and I'll show you how to do everything. Before you come, pick out the schools you want to apply to. You want a top-notch vocal program, and if possible, a winning tennis team. You major in vocal music and play on the collegiate tennis team. Your grades and ACT scores earn you a scholarship to study music. The tennis scholarship also goes toward your music education. I'm positive you could earn another scholarship with your voice. You should be able to win a full ride including room and board."

Still skeptical, Pam continues, "On one of my more courageous days, I checked into the vocal scholarship. I ran into the same obstacle again, money. I found out I need to submit a demo tape of my singing doing all types of music. The singing's not a problem but the accompaniment is. I talked to Mr. Blair, the A Cappella teacher, and he encouraged me to apply. He thinks I have enough talent he has been giving me vocal lessons before school for the past two years without my parents knowing. But he also said the quality of the recording and your accompanist either make or break you. Paul has state of the arts recording equipment to do the job, but I have no way to hire an accompanist. I have no money of my own."

I can feel my excitement growing as I try to get the words out while my mind is racing. "You've already hired one. I'll trade you the clothes for the background music. Providing you think I'm good enough."

Pam has tears in her eyes as she speaks, "Oh Terry. I can't ask you to do that; you're a concert pianist."

"I want to be but, I don't think I am at that level yet."

"You've been there since you were in grade school. The teachers called you a child prodigy. I remember when you gave concerts to the whole school. I wanted so badly to make music as you did. I begged and begged my father to get a piano. He said I was a tennis player, not a musician. A piano was a waste of money; all my time needed to be spent on the court. The day I remember the most was when you and your mother played four-hands on the piano. I thought it was the neatest thing I had ever heard. The inside of me burns to express myself through music."

"Pam, if you think I am that good, then I definitely should be the one to accompany you. If we make it a deal, it would be easier to feel like I'm not taking a handout. I would be earning my way. It's important to me and my brothers. You're easy to play for because you feel what you sing. There are also a couple of fringe benefits. The practice will help me, and didn't you say Paul would do the recording." We both laugh at the last statement. Then I add with a somber tone, "This agreement has to be tentative. Nothing's for sure until I find out about my arm. But if all goes well, a vocal scholarship is in your pocket.

Pam starts and comes out of a dream world, "I need to feed our rescue fire." She runs out of the cave. She is out of breath when she comes back in, "The fire is burning bright, and the smoke is filling the sky. Terry, you need another drink so I can fill your bottle again." I pick up the bottle and drink, surprised I am still thirsty.

When she returns, I have another question waiting, "Are you never going to play tennis again?"

"I don't know" Pam sighs, "There would have to be some tremendous changes made."

I jumped on that, "Would you ever consider playing doubles?"

Pam looks intently at me, "I would only consider it if my partner were the same caliber of player, you are, and I don't know anyone like that."

I can hardly stand the excitement, "What if I was your partner?"

Tears fill Pam's eyes again, "Are you serious?"

"I have never been more serious in my life, although it may still depend upon my arm. Coach Roy, our high school coach, told my brother if we play doubles, we stand a chance of placing in the National Armature Championships next fall. I also need a practice partner who can challenge me." Pam is speechless, and I can see I need to change the conversation, "I think we could eat the rest of the rattler now." Pam turns and wipes her eyes as she moves to the back of the cave to get our lunch.

After lunch, another bottle of water, and a willow bark pain pill, I watch as Pam starts to leave the cave with an empty water bottle and turn back. "I've been thinking, I have painted a negative picture of my parents.

They aren't all bad. They love me and have given me a special life filled with opportunities. They are good people at heart, and I do love them. I'm just ready to become my own person and control my own life." With that, she walks out into the sunlight.

I am in deep contemplation when Pam returns with the water. "You look like you're consecrating in the middle of an AP Test. What's storming in that head of yours?"

I open my eyes and decide to share my turmoil with Pam. "For the longest time I have been growing two feelings inside, one of anger and the other of emptiness. I figured out the emptiness; it came when I started pushing God out of my life. It's now beginning to lessen thanks to you and God's hand in our survival so far. The anger I can't put my finger on. For the longest time, I thought it was feeling like you were better than me, and the anger would go away if I could be better than you in every way. I know now we make much better friends than opponents, but the ugly anger is still there. I don't know where it's coming from, and I don't know how to get rid of it."

Pam moves to sit next to me and puts her hand on my good hand. "Oh, Terry, I am so sorry." Pausing to look at me she hesitates before speaking, "Do you remember our *friendly debate*?" I duck my head in total embarrassment. "I want to tell you what you taught me that day. When you started talking about that drunk driver who killed your parents, your whole appearance changed. You had the darkest most vicious feelings of hatred pouring from you. Everyone in the room could feel it."

"Pam, I do hate that man. He ruined my life.!"

"I can see why you would hate him but let me tell you what I discovered. As I felt your dark angry feelings, I recognized they were not new to me. I was growing similar resentment. My hate was growing toward my parents and their stupid controls. I thought about it often after our class. Your hate was so black and ugly, I didn't want mine to grow any larger. I didn't know what to do about it, so I talked with my seminary teacher."

"What did he tell you?" I ask.

"He told me I had to forgive my parents. He then gave me scriptures to read and pray about. He ended our conversation by challenging me to do two things. First, I was to ask in prayer if I should forgive my parents. He then said I needed to pray with real intent and ask for the Savior's help to get rid of my anger."

I ask, "Did you do it?"

"No, I wasn't quite sure how to do it, but the next day the Lord gave me more answers to my question. Steve, a guy in my seminary class, came in as mad as a hornet. He started raving about how one of his supposed good friends had just played a practical joke on him and had ruined the seat covers in his car by smearing them with raw eggs. The bell rang to start class, but the teacher let him continue venting. When he slowed down a little, he began devising plans to get even. Kids in the class were giving him horrid suggestions for more vicious get-backs.

"The teacher finally stepped to the front of the class, raised his arms in the air, and yelled, 'Stop! This is not the Savior's way. You must forgive him!'"

"Everyone in the class was surprised the teacher would take the malicious person's side. Then the teacher said, 'Steve, you must forgive so you can be healed.' Then he asked him if all his anger hurt the guilty party. Steve thought for a minute and said probably not. The teacher said everything which Steve was feeling and which he had helped the class members to feel, did not affect the prankster. The targeted boy didn't even know it was happening; he might be going on his merry way playing rotten pranks on other of his friends. Steve asked, 'What do I do then, just forget about it like it never happened?' The teacher said, 'No, you give it away to the Savior and use His Atonement to find peace. You simply pray and ask the Savior to be this guy's judge and deal with him as the Savior thinks best, so you don't have to worry about it anymore. That's why the Savior said we must forgive everyone. It's for us; not for the bad guy. Anger distances you from the Lord and the Holy Spirit. The bad guy faces the Savior's judgments and punishments. If you get even, you are as bad as or worse than your tormentor'."

"Terry, could the anger and hate you are growing be for the drunk driver that killed your parents?"

I grip Pam's hand tight and moan, "That must be it, but I don't know what to do about it. I hate him more every day."

"Terry, you need to let go of it, you have to forgive him before he kills you too."

I pull my hand back and look at Pam in stunned shock, "You don't understand; he just can't get away with killing my parents."

Pam grabs my hand again and says, "I now understand how to let the Savior deal with my problem. These last two days have taught me what it is to pray with real intent. To have peace I must give my parent problem to the Savior, and you must give the punishment of the drunk driver into His hands.

"Terry, try the advice my teacher gave me. Ask in prayer if you should forgive the drunkard and if the answer is yes, plead for His help to take it from your mind. Pray He will help you control your thoughts growing your anger and hate."

I grip Pam's hand tight and slowly begin to feel a warm light wash over me melting the anger. All I can do is cry. Pam squeezes my hand and then pulls hers away. As she gets up, she announces, "I have to go get you some more water." I begin a much-needed not so silent prayer of real intent from the far reaches of my aching soul. After all my tears are spent, a new peace lulls me to sleep.

When I awake again, Pam is sitting across the fire making more twine. I can also tell the shadows are turning to late afternoon outside the cave. I look at Pam, "Sorry I haven't been much of a survival partner."

Pam smiles and replies, "From everything I've heard about survival, we are living in style, and most of that is because of you. I found the dead stinging nettle stalks you said made thinner and stronger strings, and I've been working on them. See, I even tied my trophy to the end of one of my braids. With no doubt, I won this trophy all on my own...well maybe with a lot of help from heaven." I look closely and then laugh. There on the end of Pam's braid proudly displayed are the rattles from her conquered snake tied on with the fine twine she had just made.

Pam smiles and says, "Terry, I have another question for you. Would you be the accompanist for the A Cappella Choir next year?

I wrinkle my nose, "Where did that question come from? You're asking a lot; they sing such simplified music. You sing so well I don't even know why you're in that choir."

"Terry for being so on top of everything thing, sometimes you're clueless. Mr. Blair is the top vocal teacher in the state. He has taught the kids in the choir to sing, especially the boys. He is dedicated to helping everyone who wants to sing. We perform the songs we do because it's all the accompanists can play. We can sing a cappella but we need a piano player who can play all the parts at the same time. All our accompanists are only students from the choir with a few years of piano lessons.

"Do you remember in junior high whenever you were around a piano, you would play for kids to sing? I watched with so much longing, especially when you started teaching them to sing harmony. I would have given anything to be part of that group, but they were all boys, our competition was getting fiercer, and my dad made me spend every spare minute hitting a tennis ball. Those boys are now all in A Capella because of you. You could give them the opportunity to shine, and I could be part of it this time. If you were our accompanist, we would take state, put on standing-room-only concerts, and have a blast doing it. You can play better one-handed than any accompanist we've ever had."

I sit with my mouth open staring at Pam while I mentally digest the idea. "Well, I do have an open period next year, and if my hand will start working, it's going to need hours of extra practice. It would put me on a piano for an extra hour a day. Let's see if Mr. Blair wants me after the operation."

"Terry while you have been sleeping this afternoon, my mind has just been racing."

I laugh, "I can tell from your last new project. What else have you conjured up?"

Do you remember when we were in elementary school and were always meeting as the finalists in every competition?" I nod my head. "Do you have any idea why I wanted to compete against you?"

"So you could prove you were better than me? It didn't work though; most of the time it came out a tie."

"It was never my intention to beat you; I knew we would tie. I just wanted to get your attention. I was smart enough to understand that you and I were almost identical in every way except for your black curly hair and my straight blond hair. I watched you make up all sorts of new games on the playground, tease the boys unmercifully, and ask teachers questions they couldn't answer. You were having more fun than any other girls in our grade. We were so much the same, I knew if we put our minds together, we would be in blissful mischief all the time." I laugh at the image Pam is painting, and I know she's right.

"I asked my mom if I could invite you over to my house to become my friend. She told me you couldn't be my friend because your mother didn't belong to the country club. I thought that was the dumbest thing I had ever heard. I began working on my own plan.

"In my mind, I decided to get your attention in the contests. I knew that if you realized just how alike we were, you'd want to ask me to be your friend. That way I wouldn't be breaking mom's rule. The competition thing backfired on me. It became fiercer instead of friendlier. But Terry, I still want to be your friend.

"Look at what we've done working together so far at camp. We saved Whisty's life, set a team obstacle course record that no one will ever break, and together we've survived a flash flood. And we weren't even communicating.

"If we were friends, we would put our heads together instead of sparing. Think of what we could do. We could make our senior year one our school will never forget. I don't want to be Miss America like my mom is planning or the Wimbledon pro like my dad is counting on. I want to do something meaningful with my life helping people, and I want to start this fall."

I'm blown away by Pam's revelation. I have no reason to doubt her sincerity after the last three days. "I'm sorry Pam, I've been so clueless. When I drove the Lord's influence out of my life, I functioned pretty much on a turned-in level. What you're saying rings true. It even feels like my future depends on us being friends."

"It's not just your future Terry, it's both of our futures." Pam emphatically says.

I am about to say more when we both hear a voice outside, "Hello the fire, is anybody here." Pam flies out of the cave to the fire on the shelf. Mrs. Scott's head is peering over the ledge looking around. When she sees Pam, she turns her head and yells to someone below, "They are up here and alive. She turns her head back, "Pam, don't just stand there help me up!"

Pam kneels to grab one of her arms and her eyes fill with tears. She says in a sobbing voice, "You are where I was when the flash flood hit us. Terry dropped flat and held on to me from up here, and we were both slid along this shelf. We were being pulled into the snarling waters when a heavenly power stopped us and boosted me up until Terry could help me get up on this ledge."

CHAPTER 13

By the time Pam finishes reliving her flood experience, four more people are standing on the top of the rock pile peering over the ledge, Dixie and three Forest Rangers. One of the Rangers gives Mrs. Scott a knee to stand on, and Pam helps pull her up on the shelf. She immediately pulls Pam into a bear hug, and they cry on each other's shoulders. When they finally break their hug, she takes hold of Pam's shoulders and pushes her to an arm's length to look her over for injuries. Finally, she says "Pam, are you alright?" Pam nods her head to say yes, and Mrs. Scott reaches for the end of her braid and shakes the rattlesnake rattles. "You do have tales to tell don't you." Pam again nods her head in the affirmative. By now all four of the others are standing on the ledge.

One of the Rangers looks around awestruck, "What an oasis. No one would ever have found you here; none of us even knew this paradise existed."

Pam is intently listening to every word, "How did you find us then?"

Mrs. Scot answers for everyone, "A search plan spotted your fire this morning. The water was too high then to get to you. The pilot informed us he flew back over three more times, and the fire was still burning bright and putting out lots of smoke. With the water so high, we knew someone had to be trapped down here. We prayed it was you because the Forest Service knew of no other missing persons. I am so grateful you are alive. Where is Terry?"

"She is in our cave Mrs. Scott, and she is not doing very well. While she was holding on to me during the flash flood, something hit her arm below the elbow and cut her to the bone. It also cut the radial artery. As soon as we were out of the water, I put pressure on the cut to get the bleeding stopped, but she lost a lot of blood in the process. I bandaged it with our 104s and put her arm in a sling. I've tried to keep her hydrated and not moving much most of the time, but she needs to be in a hospital as soon as possible."

Dixie couldn't wait any longer, "Take us to her!"

Pam turns and leads the whole group to our cave. Pam points to the entrance and says, "Welcome to the George Mansion", and leads everyone inside. I am excited to tears to see everyone, but I am so weak, that I can't get up. Dixie moves to sit beside me on my right side and puts her arm around my shoulder and cries. I have as many tears running down my cheeks as she does.

One of the Rangers takes over, turning to another Ranger with a radio,

"Let all the search parties know we have found the girls, and they are alive and safe. Call headquarters and let them know we need an air evacuation helicopter. One of the girls has a severely cut arm and has sustained a large loss of blood." The Ranger with the radio steps outside the cave to make his calls and returns in about five minutes to let everyone know the chopper will be here in about twenty minutes. He also comments that our green meadow is the only place for miles where a helicopter could land in this canyon area.

After looking around the cave, the last Ranger exclaims, "How did you ever get here anyway? I thought you were on your way to Big Spring." Pam and I look at each other.

I am about to speak when Pam takes the words away. "It was a Comedy of Errors." I nod my head in agreement and decide that's a great answer for now.

The Ranger goes on to say, "Whatever your reasons for being here, it saved your lives. None of the canyons, including the main canyon, between Big Spring and the parking lot, have a place you could have climbed to escape the flood. You are two miles beyond Big Spring." Pam and I roll our eyes at each other.

Mrs. Scott is thoughtfully looking around. "This is quite a place, but I don't understand the George Mansion title."

With a smug grin, I explain, "George is the name we gave the cougar who was the former proprietor of this cave. Pam didn't appreciate his company in the middle of the night, so she chased him away throwing fireballs at him. He hasn't dared come back. Pam, why don't you take this awesome group of people back to the spring and show them what a perfect survival spot we climbed into? I'll just wait right here for my ride." Everyone but Dixie follows Pam out into the meadow. Pam has the empty water bottle in her hand.

"I am so, so glad you're alive, Terry," Dixie says with her arm still around my shoulder. "I have been so worried about you and Pam. When your bodies weren't found anywhere downstream, we figured you must have found high ground. I don't know how many times you asked me about a flash flood in the canyons, and I just shook it off. I am so thankful you are ok. How did you do the survival part with only one hand?

"Pam was my hands, and she did it well. Better than I would have done if I were in her shoes. She is great; I stopped counting how many times she saved my life."

The group makes its way back into the cave about the time everyone can hear the helicopter. Pam kneels by my side and extends her hand, "There are two pain pills left. You had better take them before you start your trip. Here is your full water bottle, take it too. I don't want you to get more dehydrated on the way home."

She hesitates and reaches to unbuckle the belt holding my knife. "Terry, I don't think I'll be needing this any longer, you better take it with you."

I grab her hand before she can release the belt. "We're not through with your survival lessons yet. You still have three weeks of camp left;

you might need it. Besides, I want you to have it as a reminder of your first successful survival trip." I pause as another idea flies into my head. "Pam in my suitcases back at Lightning Mountain, there are field guides to plants. Take them and some of your interested campers and see how many of the plants around camp you can identify. Once you know what a plant is by name, look in the edible wildlife plant book to see if you can eat it. Don't have too much fun without me."

She leans close to my ear and says, "I'm praying for you, and us."

Dixie moves out of the way, and two of the Rangers move to my sides. They carefully pick me up in their arms and carry me to the arriving chopper. I look into Pam's eyes as we pass and whisper, "You will never know how much I appreciate you. Thank you for saving me from me."

While we wait for the chopper to land, I ask the question I am almost afraid to voice. Pam gives her full attention to hear the answer when she hears me ask, "How is the rest of the camp? Did everyone make it through the flood?"

Dixie grabs my good hand and squeezes it tight as she answers, "It was a pretty scary time. We were all at Big Spring in camp wondering about you two when the wall hit. We were up high enough that water only covered everything about a foot deep. It was so spread out it didn't have much force, but it sure got everything wet. The Forest Service knew we were in there and in trouble. They brought their handy helicopter in and transported the whole wet mess down to the trail's end in a few trips. No one was hurt, and everything dried out quickly. The worst part was worrying about you two. Everyone searched the best they could with the high water. One of your packs was found about two miles below the parking lot. We debated and debated if it was a good sign or a bad one. The only thing giving us hope was your bodies hadn't been found. We knew if you were alive, you would survive. Looks like we were right."

The chopper hovers for an instant and then sits down in the center of the meadow. The engine keeps running, and the blades continue turning as the doors open and a hand beckoned everyone to come. We move as a group to the waiting machine, and one at a time climb aboard. I am lifted from hands on the ground to hands in the helicopter. I take one last glance around to say goodbye to my first real survival experience. When my eyes pass the spring, a hand rests on my shoulder and squeezes. It's Pam. As soon as I'm buckled into my seat, I am asleep.

I vaguely remember the helicopter setting down and Pam touching my arm. I try to wake up, and I think Pam is talking to me. "Good luck, Terry. We'll be praying for you lots." It seems there is more, but it's lost to sinking sleep.

The chopper stops long enough to drop off the rangers, Pam, and Dixie. Mrs. Scott stays on board with me. Once we are in the air again, one of the two men flying the craft turns to Mrs. Scott. He yells loudly to be heard above the roar of the craft.

"We've been in contact with the hospital in the closest town. We've advised them of your situation, and they say they are not equipped to help your girl. If it's okay with you, we'll fly her home." Mrs. Scott nods approval twice and the pilot goes on. "We'll alert the University Hospital, and they will have their specialist waiting. It'll take us about three hours. You better follow your girl's example and get some rest."

I try to shake loose from the deep fog that's surrounding me to respond to whomever is calling my name. Finally, I recognize Mrs. Scott's voice. "Terry! Terry, wake up. When you sleep, you really sleep. You need to wake up and get ready to get off."

I slowly came too and happen to glance out the window. Even though it is dark, the sight brings me quickly awake. We are over a city, and if I'm not mistaken, it's my city. I look out intently. When I recognize where we are, I turn to Mrs. Scott. "I'm home. How did we get here so fast? Are we going to the University Hospital? Will my brother be there?"

Mrs. Scott cuts me off before I can ask another question. "Slow down a little. Yes, you are home. Yes, that's the University Hospital. And yes, your brother, Tom, has been contacted. He should be here." I have no time to talk further as we touch down on the landing pad.

Before the door is opened by the hurrying hospital attendants, the pilot says to Mrs. Scott, "We'll be heading back as soon as you get this young lady into good hands, and you know she's well taken care of. I assume you want to ride back with us."

Mrs. Scott thanks them for their help and concern and says she would like very much to ride back with them. Their conversation has hardly ended when an attendant dressed in pale green climbs aboard and moves right to me. As he unbuckles my safety straps, he asks, "Can you walk out, or should we carry you?"

I look at the short distance between me and the door, "I think I can walk to the door if you hold on to me. It's my arm that's hurt, not my feet." With his help, I maneuver out of my seat to the door, and then I'm lifted down into the waiting wheelchair by two of my brothers. The attendant then pushes the wheelchair followed by my three brothers straight to the Emergency Room.

A dignified, gray-haired man is sitting on the patient's gurney and smiles when they roll me in. "I'm Dr. Haden. I've been told you and I should have a little get-together. How can I help you?"

I like this man right away. He is soothingly calm after all the semi-frantic people I have encountered in the past few hours. I point to my bandaged arm, "I have a little cut on this arm, and my hand doesn't work anymore."

The doctor gently takes hold of my clenched fist, "What happens if you try and open your hand?"

I grimace at the thought of even trying. "It sends all kinds of shooting pains up my arm, and the hand just sits there."

He then extends one of my fingers and pokes it with a pin as Pam had done. "What do you feel when I do that?"

I smart from the pain. "It still feels like I'm being used for a pincushion. My friend who bandaged my arm did the same thing." I catch my word. Friend, is that ever an about-face!

I have no time to ponder any implications. The doctor is waiting for his next answer. "How deep is your cut? Did you see it?"

My stomach turns over as I recall my first glance at my arm. "It goes clear to the bone, and blood was squirting all over. I couldn't believe I didn't feel it until we were out of the water, and Pam saw it."

"You mean you were in the water when this happened?"

I relate the whole experience to him starting with our panicked run for the promising rockslide. When I finish, he says "It sounds to me like you're more than lucky to be alive."

He seems to have received all the information he needs. He stands and begins to make things happen. "We need to check and see how much blood you've lost. After the lab pokes its needle in you, the nurses will help you get ready. We're scheduled to be in surgery in five minutes." Moving toward the door he adds, "I need to get scrubbed. I'll meet you in the operating room. Don't take off your bandage; I'll do it when you're under." With that, he disappears into the busy hall.

Alone with my brothers for the first time, I start to cry. All my brothers start talking at once. Tom tries to come to my aid. "Terry, we're so glad you're okay. We've been going crazy since we were notified you were caught in the flash flood. We knew if you were not killed you could survive anything-"

Then Randy asks, "We all know you're the survival queen, but how did you do it with one hand?"

"I used Pam's hands. I'll tell you all about it later, but right now I don't have much time. Will you all give me a blessing before I go to surgery? And please bless me to be able to use my hand again." My brothers all look like they have a million questions but quickly move to put their hands on my head. They have just finished the prayer when the nurse comes through the door with my new wardrobe.

My brothers are going out the door so I can dress when Randy turns and says, "Rick and I will stay until we know the outcome of your surgery. If everything goes well, we'll head back to our schools. We both have work and finals starting tomorrow. We will all be praying for you. We love you!"

Again, I fight the formidable task of trying to wake up. I almost make it to consciousness level several times and then slip away again. When I finally open my eyes, I am in a hospital room, and Tom is in the chair beside my bed. When he sees my eyes flicker, he comes to his feet. "Welcome home Terry. This is hardly how I expected you to come back from camp, but I'm so thankful you're okay. I have never prayed so hard in my life—It has surely taken you a long time to wake up. Your surgery was yesterday."

I am still fighting the effects of the anesthetic mixed with my loss of blood exhaustion, but I finally become fully conscious. "Hi Tom," I say as I try to gather my thoughts. "Have I been asleep since yesterday? Did Randy and Rick leave?"

Then the full impact of my situation sinks in. "How did the surgery go anyway? Will my hand work again?"

Tom smiles as he looks past me to the door. "Why don't you ask the man who knows?"

My eyes follow Tom's to the figure walking in. He speaks before I can recognize him. "I'm glad to see you're finally awake. You and I had quite a time together in the operating room. You even talk when you're under. Someday I'd like to know about George. You just kept saying over and over, 'Is George out there? I know he's out there. I can hear him. Put more wood on the fire.' This George must be quite a character."

I blush with embarrassment but don't say a word about George. Instead, I jump immediately to the pressing issue on my mind. I look down at the bandage which limits all movement and engulfs my hand and arm, "Will I be able to use it again?"

"I've never seen a closer 'yes' in all my operating days. The tendons and muscles were completely cut, but we could sew them back together. The real worry was the radial nerve. It was hanging by a microscopic thread. You owe a great deal to whomever fixed you up. With the bandaging and the sling, they immobilized your arm enough, so the stress was taken off the nerve. If you'd have tried to use it at all, it would have pulled apart, and there would have been nothing we could do. As it is, the nerve has already started to repair its sheath. As soon as the muscles heal, you'll have a little physical therapy to do. In a couple of months, you may be a little stiff in the mornings, but you'll be as good as new." With a grin he adds. "You'll even have to go back to piano practicing."

I feel good. I don't care how long it takes as long as there is a way to get back the use of my hand. Then the doctor's last comment registers. I look at him with questioning eyes, "How do you know I play the piano?"

Doctor Harden winks at Tom, "I talked with your brother while we were waiting for you to fly in. He told me of your dream to win the music scholarship and be a concert pianist. I told him we'd do everything humanly possible. I did my job, but as I said before, the biggest credit goes to your original nurse. She also saved your life as well as your hand. I could tell when I got inside your arm the radial artery had also been cut severely. You could have bled to death if you hadn't received some good attention." He picks up my chart and continues, "I think we're through with you. You can go home this afternoon. You need to take it easy for a few days. You know, sleep, lie around, and sleep. We gave you extra plasma, but your body still needs to build its blood back up before you'll have all your energy back. See me in my office in two weeks."

He turns and heads to the door. I manage to get one word to stop him, "Wait! —How long until I can use it?"

The doctor smiles, "Six weeks in this bandage/cast with no movement. Then you will start physical therapy and use your fingers on the piano."

"What about tennis?" I quickly interject.

The doctor wrinkles his forehead, "You athletes are all the same. When can I get back on the field or the court? Six weeks of no movement until I take off the cast. If everything looks good, then you can start swinging your racket and practicing the piano. However, I can't caution you enough to go easy. You can work through tightness but not through pain. It will cause you to build scar tissue which will limit your piano playing."

I lower my head a little, "I promise to go easy; I have too much to lose if I don't. Thank you from the bottom of my heart."

The doctor smiles, "I'll see you in two weeks."

I decide I must have been more worried about my arm than I realized. The peace I feel right at this moment is wonderful. My mind begins to wander back to the three days of survival when Tom interrupts my travels. "Terry, you have to see the front page of the paper. You're a hero. Listen to this. 'Terry Masters Pulls Fellow Camper from Flash Flood.' It goes on to say—" Before he can even finish the sentence, I pull the paper from his hands and continue reading in silence.

When I finish, I wave the paper in agitation. "She can't do that. It's not fair."

Tom's bewildered as he watches me. "Isn't the article right? Didn't you pull her out of the flood?"

I go on trying to make Tom understand. "Sure, I held on to her and helped pull her out of the water, but that was after she boosted me up on the ledge. It doesn't say anything about her saving my life, the bleeding, the cougar, or the rattlesnake. All this paper talks about is me being the hero."

Tom takes advantage of my deep breath to sneak into the

231

conversation. "Terry, think about it. If someone were interviewing you, would you tell them how you rescued Pam, or would you tell them about the things Pam did for you?"

I know Tom is right, but it still didn't make it right. This means no one at camp even knows the whole story. Getting hold of Mrs. Scott becomes my biggest priority before the last night of camp. I am about to devise a method to do this when Tom interrupts my thoughts again. "I think it's up to you to let the world know the rest of the story. Whom are you most concerned about knowing there are two sides after you tell me?"

I answer with no hesitation, "The staff at Lightning Mountain."

Tom nods his head. "That makes sense. I guess you'll have to set them straight when we go up there in three weeks."

Tom says it so matter of factly it takes a full second to register what he's said. When it does, I scream. "Oh Tom, do you mean it?"

"I'm already scheduled to be off work to go down and pick you up. I figure you would still like to be there for the last night and the Awards Program. I know I want to be there." With a smirk, he adds, "If you don't want to go with me, I'll find someone to stay here and take care of you while I go."

I want to throw something at him and hug him at the same time. All I can get out is, "Thank you, Tom. You'll never know how much it means for me to be there for the last night."

Tom gets up and moves toward the door. "You get dressed and get your things together. I'll go see what I have to do to bail you out of here."

I sink back on the pillow with a sigh. Hospital bill! I think we have insurance, but I'm not sure it will even come close to covering the cost of a specialist like Dr. Haden. The rule has always been, that *we must stay healthy because we can't afford to get sick.* Until now, no one has had any major medical needs. I begin to feel a little sick at the prospects ahead.

I haven't moved when Tom walks back in the door. "You must like this place. Don't you want to go home?" I am about to protest when Tom says. "Do you know a Mr. D. Fletcher?"

I look at him questioningly and answer, "It would have to be Pam's father. Why?"

I can't read the look on Tom's face as he speaks. "He paid your hospital bill."

CHAPTER 14

Even though I fill my time with sleeping, eating, sleeping, sleeping, visiting with friends who drop in, and one-handed piano playing, it seems like the longest three weeks I have ever lived. I arrange my pillows in the back seat, while the morning is not yet beginning to turn gray. I feel strange as I try to put a name to my emotions. I feel as if I should be at camp, yet the last week has felt unreal. Waking up and finding I am home seems as if I am in a dream I can't get out of. Whatever my emotions, I'm glad to be going back to camp.

Tom puts the last of our things in the car and buckles himself into the driver's seat. It is early enough I decide to start in the back seat where I can stretch out. Before Tom can start the car, I put my hand on his shoulder and softly ask, "Would it be all right if we have a prayer before we go?

Tom turns as far as his seat belt will let him go. "Terry, you never cease to amaze me. You know I would love to have a prayer with you. Someday, you're going to have to tell me everything that happened to you in that canyon." I just smile and nod my head.

As we back out of the driveway, I ask, "It's a long drive. Are you going to be okay if I don't talk and keep you awake?"

Tom looks at me in the rearview mirror. "I was going to make this trip alone, remember? When I get tired, I'll stop. Besides, I don't think you'll sleep all the time, will you?"

I smile to myself as I answer, "We'd get there faster if I did."

Tom mumbles as we pull onto the interstate. "I think it takes me as long to get there whether you sleep or not."

We have only been going for less than fifteen minutes when I feel myself growing drowsy. I think to myself before I drift out, if I sleep most of the way, I sure hope my body will have enough energy to do something besides sleep once I get there.

I oscillate between sleep and talk, with an emphasis on sleeping, the whole trip back to camp. In the late afternoon, when we round the last bend and drive into the parking lot, it feels as though I have never left. I am out of the car before Tom brings it to a stop. I call back to him as I hurry toward the lodge. "Make yourself at home. I've got to find Mrs. Scott before the dinner meal starts. If I don't catch her before, there will be no chance before the Awards Program tonight." I hear Tom comment, but I am too far away to be sure and feel too pressured for time to go back.

I move as straight to the office as I can. I'm stopped by every camper and staff member I meet to find out how I am. I answer all of them with a quick, "I'm great. Have you seen Mrs. Scott?" hoping they'll sense my urgency. It seems to work, for each sends me on my way with instructions to check the office, Mrs. Scott was last seen there.

At last, I reach the camp director's door and knock. Holding my breath, I wait for a reply. When I am about to give up and turn away, a voice calls from the inside, "You don't have to knock, just come in."

My stomach is in knots again. Why is it always so hard to talk to this lady? I take another deep breath and walk through the door. Mrs. Scott is working on papers at her desk and doesn't look up until I start to speak. "Mrs. Scott, do you have a—"

That's all I get out before she jumps to her feet and has me captured in a careful huge hug. "Terry, we've been so worried about you. How are you? How's your hand? I wanted so much for you to be here tonight, but I never dreamed you'd make it. How did you get here?"

Mrs. Scott moves us both to a couch to sit down. My head spins as I try to decide which question to answer first. Then I think of my urgent message. "I'm fine. My hand's going to be as good as new. That's what I want to talk to you about before tonight."

Mrs. Scott looks as though she wants to say more, but she says, "Go ahead. I'm listening."

I pull out the folded newspaper clipping Tom had shown me the day after surgery. "I read this article when I was in the hospital. When I first read it, I was frustrated. This is not even half the story. Then I decided there wasn't anyone around, namely me, to tell the other half. I don't know what Pam's told you. If it's anything like what I read in the paper, it's only a small part. I'd like a chance to tell you everything that happened."

Mrs. Scott doesn't say anything. She only looks intently at me. I take this as a go-ahead signal and start explaining. I share with her the major points of our adventure beginning with the communication blackout on the trip downstream, my trailblazing up the wrong canyon, and my lack of attention to the weather as the clouds gathered. I talk about all the things Pam did to make our survival possible and about each time she saved my life. I end with what Dr. Harden had said about her saving my hand and my life.

Mrs. Scott thinks a moment and asks, "Terry, why is it so important I know all of this right now?"

I am sure Mrs. Scott knows, but she is going to make me say it anyway. I fish for a detour but find no approach but the direct one. "I'm quite sure Pam and I are competing for the Silver Dove Award tonight. I wanted you to know all the details before dinner so you can talk to the selections committee before the program. I think Pam should get the award." I said it, and it felt good. Now, I can relax and enjoy my last night at camp.

"Terry, I have a question for you. I knew you were the most skilled individual here this summer, but when did you become so proficient in survival skills?"

I wonder what that has to do with our conversation, but I quickly answer. "Before my mom and dad were killed, you might say wilderness survival was their work escape passion. We practiced survival skills at least once a week during the year, and in the summer, our vacations were to go to a different spot each year and live off the land surviving for two weeks or more. It was so ingrained in my brothers, that after the accident, we just kept up the tradition. You could put any one of us anywhere and we could survive for a month or more."

I have another question Terry, "Did Pam have survival skills?"

Now I am more puzzled, "I don't think she ever had the chance to learn survival, but she sure was a fast learner. I couldn't do anything with my arm, so she just kept asking me what she should do next. She was my hands. She is smart, but what's better is she quickly understands how to apply what she learns to new situations. She also creatively thinks on her own. When that rattlesnake crawled up on my rock to sit beside me, I couldn't say a word. Pam just analyzed the problem and quickly took care of it. She saved my life repeatedly. That's why I think she should receive the Silver Dove award tonight."

Mrs. Scott's expression doesn't change. She just looks at me. When she finally speaks it is more matter of fact than I expect. "Thank you, Terry. I'll see to it the selection committee considers all aspects of the award. I'm sure your unit will be glad to see you back, even if it's only for one night. I'm overjoyed to see you back too and especially thankful you will have the use of your hand again."

I know our conversation is over, and I walk out the door. I now understand what it is, and why I always feel uncomfortable talking to the Camp Director. When I'm finished, I feel as if what I have said has little or no impact on an already predetermined decision. I feel good about following through with my plan, though. I said what I needed to say.

Standing on the stairs to the lodge, I grin from ear to ear as I form a new thought. My plan needs one more phase. If I am awarded the Silver Dove tonight instead of Pam, I will make my own award presentation and give it to her right there. They always give the recipient a chance to say a few words. I will let the whole camp know what Pam did and then give her the award. With that resolve, I float down the stairs and head toward the noisy campers gathering for the flag ceremony.

As soon as the Adventurers spot me, they engulfed me in a whirlwind of excitement. They ask so many questions and make so much noise no one can hear a thing. The flag ceremony is five minutes late starting because no one can quiet the Adventurers down. Dinner isn't much better. If anyone from outside our unit had wanted to even approach me, it would have been impossible. The campers want to be as close as possible, and they share me with no one. I look around for Pam from time to time but never catch a glimpse of her. Again, I feel a strange contradiction inside. Here I am back in camp and trying to find Pam instead of avoiding her.

After dinner, we return to our unit so the girls can show me all the things they have been doing since I left. I'm given a grand tour through the completed postcard picture gallery. I'm impressed with the vision the girls have developed for capturing nature's beauty. Their pictures would rival any I have ever seen in a gift store. The girls crowd so closely Dixie finally makes a rule they can be near me but not touch me. I am glad Dixie shares my fear that I might get bumped or pushed and injure my arm.

The time passes fast, and before I know it, we are on our way back to the lodge with our luggage for the Awards Program. As we walk into the rearranged dining hall, campers wave to their parents who are seated in the rear of the room on benches. Each unit stays as a group and moves to the front to sit on the floor. Once the girls are settled, the camp staff move onto the small stage in front of the entire group where we are all seated in a large semi-circle. It will be a long night, but no one will mind. When the last award and speech are over the campers will join their parents and camp will be over.

Walking past the Explorer Unit seated on the floor, I notice that most of the girls are wearing braided hair. Pam must have continued with her native hairdo when she got back to camp.

When we climb onto the stage, I notice where the Explorer Staff are seated and head in that direction. I do a double-take when I see Pam. She is wearing braids again. I quickly slid into the empty seat next to her. I whispered into her ear, "Cute hair!"

Pam whispers back, "It's for you." Pam puts her arm around my shoulder and hugs me. "Terry, I'm so glad you're here. I've been praying a lot for you. How are you? How's your hand? Will you be able to use it?"

I am surprised at how choked with emotion I am when I try to speak. "Thanks to you and the Lord, I'm here, and my hand will be as good as before. The doctor said my nurse saved both my hand and my life." I try to say more but my eyes only fill with tears. I try to change the subject but don't get far-off track. "I couldn't believe it when we checked out of the hospital, and Tom found out our bill had been paid. They told him it had been taken care of by a Mr. D. Fletcher. That's your dad, isn't it?"

My eyes follow Pam's to the audience. "That's my dad. I told you he is basically a good guy. He just gets carried away with controlling and being on top, and he doesn't want to share the limelight with anybody. When he tries to live his life through me, he expects me to fill his dreams. He does have a heart of gold when he's not competing. He doesn't know quite what to do with you now. It's his way of saying thank you for saving my life."

Pam has to ask one more question, "How are you on the inside?"

I smile and whisper, "Thanks again to you and the Lord, I have peace and no anger. What about you?"

Pam whispers back, "Thanks to you and the Lord, my life now has peace and direction."

I want to talk more, but the program has already started. We are whispering to finish as much as we do. When Dixie pokes me, I know we'll have to wait for later. As I settle back to enjoy the night, I am pleased with the feeling that is still there between Pam and me. It feels so much better to be building a friendship instead of a wall.

The night lengthens as I knew it would. Everyone gets a certificate for attending Lightning Mountain Camp. Everyone also gets an individual award of some kind. There are awards for the Friendliest Camper, The

Most Energetic, The Most Helpful, and the Most Skilled Camper. There are lighter awards given for Using the Most Band-Aids, Sleepwalking the Most, and every silly thing that happens at camp. I get one for the Best Underwater Swimmer. It was given for my swim after the inner tube exploded. Pam gets the Botanist Award, for her thorough identification of all plants, particularly Poison Ivy.

The stack of award papers dwindles to zero, and everyone knows it's time for the top award of all, the Silver Dove. Mrs. Scott moves to the stage front and the awards table for her speech. In my mind, I try to give Mrs. Scott a message. Please, please give it to Pam. She earned it. She deserves it. I hold my breath again as she starts speaking.

"It's time for our last award, the Silver Dove. This award has been part of Lightening Mountain Camp since it began fifty-seven years ago. It has always been given to the camper who has proven herself over several years to have the best camping skills, the best leadership skills, and the best overall integrity. By the time a girl spends nine or ten summers with us, there is usually no decision to make as to whom should receive this award. We can usually tell at least a year in advance who will be the recipient the following year."

In an unexpected move, she turns around to face the staff and holds out her hands. "Will Pam and Terry please come forward?" I am completely taken by surprise, and I can tell by the look on Pam's face she is too. We both move to stand on either side of Mrs. Scott, where she motions us to go. My mind races, what is going on? This is completely different from any other awards night I have attended since I began coming to camp nine years ago.

When Mrs. Scott has us where she wants us, she goes on. "Nine years ago, when Terry and Pam started coming to camp, we began to observe a break in tradition. At the end of each summer, we always had two girls who were top in their age level. At the end of last summer, there were still two girls who were the best campers. As the selection committee, we knew we would have our work cut out for us this summer. We have watched very carefully, very, very carefully. At one point we watched so carefully we decided neither one of them would receive the award." I can't hide my embarrassed smile as I think back to my intense dislike for Pam, and how I had hidden my attitude so poorly. I am ashamed enough I hope no one can read my thoughts or even guess what I am thinking. "We continued watching past that point, and we still could not make the decision.

"The first night of pre-camp staff training, we were ending our day with a songfest. We sang new songs we had learned and then our favorite oldies. When we were ending, I asked Pan to sing the song she won the state vocal competition with, and Terry accompanied her. They thought they were finished, but I ask them to perform, "You Raise Me Up." The selection committee has decided we want all of you to hear this song so you will understand our decision. I know Terry will be a little handicapped, but if you close your eyes, you will never know she is only playing with one hand. Pam and Terry, will you move to the piano? All of you may sing along if you like."

Pam and I stare at each other as we begin to move. Pam whispers,

"Can you do this Terry?

I whisper as I sit down, "I can; can you?" I then move my right hand to the keys and touch them all over the keyboard. I finally look at Pam and say, "I am ready when you are."

With tears rolling down her cheeks, Pam nods her head to begin. There is absolute silence in the room, and I think, Pam if you can sing through those tears, you are a total professional, as I start the introduction. Pam lifts her head and begins to sing on exactly the right note with a beautiful tone. The emotions coming from us through our music are electrifying. No one joins in to sing, and most faces streamed with tears.

When we are finished, there is no sound or movement in the room. Everyone is spellbound. A thought strikes me like lightning, and I began the introduction to another song, "You'll Never Walk Alone." Pam turns her head, gives me a slight smile, moves to put her hand on my shoulder, and begins to sing. As Pam sings the first two notes, I realize I have pitched the song too low for her voice, and I quickly modulated it into the right key.

The audience's reaction is one of pure amazement. There is neither a sound nor a dry eye, but the emotions are now also coming from the audience. When we end this song, I immediately stand, turn, and reach to give Pam a giant one-armed hug. The audience rises to their feet and noise, clapping, shouting, and yelling shatter the room. With arms around each other's shoulders, Pam and I walk back to stand by Mrs. Scott. While the clamor is slowly dying down, Pam whispers in my ear, "Thanks for the key change.

I mumble a quick, "Just doing what I do, so you can do what you do."

Finally, Mrs. Scott has everyone's attention, but the audience remains on their feet. She begins speaking, "By a unanimous vote of the selections committee, which is the entire staff, we have decided to break with a fifty-seven-year-old tradition. Tonight, we award the Silver Dove to two girls, Pamula Fletcher and Terry Masters." The audience must have agreed because once again the noise and clapping explode. We throw our arms around each other again.

We turn to face the audience still holding one arm around each other's shoulders. I look over the entire group and then catch the expression on Mr. Fletcher's face. I lean close to Pam's ear so she can hear above the noise. "Your dad doesn't look so happy."

Pam turns to my ear to respond, "I told you he doesn't like to share the top with anyone. But it's our limelight, and I love it. He'll just have to get used to it, especially since we're going to play doubles starting as soon as you can swing a racket."

Mrs. Scott turns to stand in front of both of us, raises her voice, and leans forward so we can both hear, "Thank you for taking care of each other! You both have a place on Lightning Mountain's staff in the future if your busy lives will allow it." She hands us each a white envelope, "Here's your paycheck for your summer's AUL work. I think by saving three lives you've earned every penny of it. I learned yesterday that Whisty is well on her way to recovery without any paralysis. Thought you would like to know." She smiles, gives us both a hug, then turns away to talk to parents and campers.

Shadows In The Campus Halls
Vol. 2

CHAPTER 1

I slowly curl my left hand into a fist and slam it down on my baby grand piano keys. With tears rolling down my cheeks I yell with furry, "I can't do this!" I fold both arms in front of me, lay them not so gently on the keyboard, put my head on my arms, and sob. In my mind, I yell, "This is never going to work. I will never be able to use my hand again. The doctor was wrong. I will never play with both hands again."

I feel two hands on my shoulders, and hear Pam's gentle voice say, "Hi Terry."

I turn so fast I almost fell off the piano bench, but I can't stop sobbing. Pam takes hold of my left hand, pulls me up, and crosses the room to the couch where we both sit down.

Pam waits until I am calmed down enough that I can get out a few words. "Pam, I'm never going to be able to play the piano again. This dumb hand will not work. I will never play on a concert stage. I probably won't even be able to play tennis…"

www.ingramcontent.com/pod-product-compliance
Lightning Source LLC
LaVergne TN
LVHW010159070526
838199LV00062B/4420